AURA

Viewing • Reading • Cleansing

By

Hittesh Morjaria

EBD

EMBASSY BOOKS
www.embassybooks.in

AURA

Viewing • Reading • Cleansing

First published in India 2012

Published in India by :
EMBASSY BOOK DISTRIBUTORS
120, Great Western Building,
Maharashtra Chamber of Commerce Lane,
Fort, Mumbai - 400 023.
Tel : (+91-22) 22819546 / 32967415
Email : info@embassybooks.in
Website: www.embassybooks.in

ISBN 13: 978-93-80227-96-2

Preface

!! Guru Brahmaa, Guru Vishnu, Guru Devo Maheshwara Guruh Sakhshat Para Bhramha Tasmai Sri Guruve Namah !!

Meaning:

I prostrate to Sri Guru, who is Brahmaa, the creator; Vishnu, the sustainer, Mahesh, the destroyer and the Supreme Being.

"That which is within and around us, that which is governing our lives, that which is our nature and mind, that which can be only seen or felt by a real Yogi is Aura"

"May God be with us, within us, above us, around us. May realization dawn on us, that our Aura that is our Consciousness, which is with us, within us and around us is 'God'. Everything that is, is what we call God"

Table of Contents

SECTION
1

1. Definition of Aura

"Aum purnamadah purnamidam purnaart purna mudchayete!
Purnassaya purnamaadaya purnamevaa vashishyete !!

Aum shanti shanti shantihi !!

Meaning

Aum that 'God' is complete, this 'Me' is complete, from the complete has the complete manifested; from the complete at the time of deluge the complete is negated, what remains is complete.

Aum let peace be, let peace be, let peace be.

▶ The English dictionary describes Aura as:
✓ A distinctive atmosphere or
✓ The subtle emanation around us. The word Aura is derived from the name of the Greek goddess of breeze and atmosphere; it means an atmosphere surrounding a being.

▶ In many ancient statues and paintings of different saints, Gods, angels and prophets of different religions such as Hindu, Christian, Greek, Parsi, Jain, Buddhist etc. Aura is shown as a bright halo, which resembles their strong minds and inherent qualities.

▶ It is said that when Janaka, a learned king of Indian mythology, wanted to enquire about a dream he saw, he called upon many learned scholars, but was not satisfied. Then a person called Ashtawakra – which means a person with eight dents in his body – was summoned. Looking at Ashtawakra crawling with his dented body, people in Janaka's court started laughing. However, Janaka could recognize the Aura of Ashtawakra and with full respect and love allowed Ashtawakra to guide him to enlightenment.

▶ This whole universe is very mysterious. Our body is a bigger mystery. From what the world knows, and is now scientifically proven with the help of Kirlian cameras, etc. is that Aura is nothing but a pale electromagnetic halo-like light around and within us. It is also called Aabhaa, Tejmandal and Jalwa in different Indian languages. According to me, Aura is the **mind of a being**.

✓ In other words, Aura is the nerve centre from where thoughts, good or bad, arise and depart. It has been observed by different experts that the Aura changes its shape and colour showing a change in sensation and thinking.

✓ If you squeeze our eyes and try to look at the sun you will see strings of silver light flowing towards you. These silver rays are called Prana. Prana is the vital life force. and the source of Prana on earth is the sun. It is difficult for any life form to sustain without getting Prana. There are some life forms that receive Prana through air or water as they do not expose their bodies to the sun throughout their lives. These living beings or plants are very low in Prana and are called Tamsic (low in energy).

✓ Our Aura is made up of these very silver rays of Prana. They exists in our body in an entangled, circular floral shapes called the Chakra, around and within our body. You can say that our body is like a tree and the Aura is like a creeper that wraps around it.

✓ Your mood defines the colour of your Aura. Every colour makes it possible for the mystic to read your mind and to diagnose and repair the emotional and physical damages, as every colour tells him about what you are thinking. It also shows the damage in the body-mind system even before the symptoms make a surface in physical form.

✓ The size and the colour of the Aura, and specially the Chakra, state the nature, interest, health, mood and spiritual advancement of a person.

✓ It takes a very senior mystic, and a lot of practice, to see different layers, Chakras and colours of the Aura.

✓ Some people believe that the electromagnetic field of Aura is only around our face, **but this is not true.** Aura does not only surround our whole body, it is also within us, and it also enters the ground that you stand on, if you are not wearing energy-insulating footwear. In fact, the Aura is at its maximum intensity around your feet, followed by your palms and then around your face.

✓ The electro magnetic field of the Aura attracts and repels people from each other. This explains our likes or dislike towards a person even before we meet them.

✓ It is also observed that people start behaving differently, either consciously or subconsciously, in the presence of the opposite sex. This is also the effect of male and female opposite magnetic fields attracting each other.

✓ From time immemorial in different religions and societies, people hug, shake hands, kiss hands or touch the feet on meeting people as a gesture of greeting. This is to exchange thoughts by accepting each others' Aura.

✓ Aura gets released from the feet, so touching the feet is considered as a process of receiving blessings, or we can say to receive a part of their Aura. In India, it is considered that one must prostrate or show respect to elders or learned ones by touching their feet or joining hands before them to receive their grace, which in turn will make them like the ones they show respect to. Aura is received by the palms so shaking hands or touching of feet is done using a part of the hand, say fingers. Aura is easily exchanged through the meeting of faces. This also explains why people often greet each other by the way of a hug or a kiss on the cheek. **This instantly places two different individual on a common platform of understanding and liking.**

✓ The Aura also enters the ground that you are walking or standing on. It exchanges energy with the ground that we stand on, and this is the reason why people are often ask to walk bare foot on the grass or on wooden flooring, or atleast stay barefooted in your homes so that the stale energy of your Aura is released and replaced with fresh energy that will keep you healthy, fresh and happy. **It has been observed that people, who do not walk barefoot in their homes, get health issues like arthritis and their senses get weakened in old age.**

▶ It is not only India or the East that knew about Aura. Even the West was well informed about its existence for a long period. Lately, all the research about Aura has been derived from the west.

✓ 'Raiment' and 'Countenance of light' are the words used in the Bible for Aura.

✓ There is a place called West Kimberleys in Australia where one can find thousands of years old cave paintings showing people with a golden Aura.

✓ There are many books written on the Aura by western psychics and clairvoyants.

✓ Many western arts and traditions like Theosophy, Anthroposophy, Archeosophy etc. have done a precise research on Aura, its sizes and colours indicating different emotional, mental and physical states.

▶ Insight into the research of some western Psychis & clairvoyants.

1. Psychics and clairvoyants like Edgar Cayce have done a lot to throw enough light on this mistique subject.

2. Edgar Cayce claimed that the ability of seeing the Aura with naked eyes is weakened with age. I have not received any such complaint from Indian seekers. In-

fact a Sadhu (Indian Saint) called Ramaanand who taught me to see Aura with naked eyes was much older. So, I believe we will keep this claim of Edgar Cayce on hold till we get an old clairvoyant with this complaint or I myself wait for my turn to be old and experience it.

3. Charles Leadbeater, a western theosophist of the 19th century has given a detailed analysis of the Aura and its colour. An Italian theosophist called Palamidessi carried on further with his work on the Aura.

4. Another westerner W.E. Butler has mentioned two layers of Aura. First is clairvoyance or mental and second is ether or spiritual.

5. Robert Bruce, another westerner went a step ahead of W.E. Butler and mentioned three layers of the Aura First ether, second main and third spiritual.

6. He also came out with revolutionary researches against some orthodox beliefs, such as that the Aura cannot be seen in complete darkness, as it was perceived by many.

7. Secondly the Aura cannot be seen unless some portion of the person or object emitting the Aura is not seen. This is partly correct. By experience, I will like to add that a person's Aura can be seen and also cleansed in his photograph or in the unwashed clothes that the person has used.

8. Inventions of latest gadgets like the kirlian camera and different computer hardwares and softwares for Aura reading is the latest contribution to this mystique art by the west (see picture elsewhere in the book).

2. The Basic Principles of Aura

"The most beautiful thing we can experience is the mystical.
It is the source of all true art and science."

Albert Einstein

The Aura which is our mind is seen in everyone and everything. It is said in the scriptures, that everything that is in motion so every thing is alive and has a mind and feelings; but everything is vibrating at different frequencies, hence they have different sizes or Kala of the Aura. Non-living thing things are at a lesser frequency and living things are at a higher frequency.

▶ **Living and Non-living**

✓ It has been observed that Aura is present in living beings as well as non living objects.

✓ This leads to an important question: How can a non-living object have a mind if we claim that the Aura is a state of the mind ?

✓ Modern science now believes what the Indian scriptures have said ages ago that nothing is static. Everything, every atom is in motion.

✓ Motion means life and static means death or non living. So by this definition, we come to an understanding that everything is living in this universe. Whether or not that 'being' is aware of its own existence depends on the level at which its mind has been developed. It also depends on how big is its Aura, or at what speed its atoms and molecules are vibrating.

✓ Although this might sound absurd, let me remind you that in the past, science believed that plants are non-living things too. At the time, the saying from the ancient Hindu scriptures that "plants are living and they have emotions like pain, sorrow, happiness, fear etc., or they can communicate with us" would have sounded absurd, but today criminal cases have been solved with the help of plants displaying their emotions in the West.

✓ Also, we all have experienced that entering a certain place or wearing a certain thing or specific colour cloth can change our mood pattern. This explains that everything has an Aura, a mind of its own. The Aura of the place or the thing gets affected by the Aura of the beings around it or using it (we will elaborate more on this in the chapters to come), and in return they affect everything, which comes within their Aura. This is based on the principle of relativity that every thing is affected and is affecting everything else.

▶ Attributes

"You think you are living in this universe,
within the limits of your mind and body,
NO. I say this universe and many others are
just a fraction of your imagination and so also ? within your mind."

'Hittesh Morjaria'

✓ There are twenty-three attributes or forms of energy, of which the whole universe is made of and these twenty three attributes are also present in our body and Aura.

✓ We are governed by our mind, our Aura, which is subtle, form of energy, and that in turn is ruled by something, which is even more subtle —— the attributes by which it is made.

✓ Our Aura 'governs' and also 'reflects' our health, mental and emotional state. It also is a window that shows an oncoming illnes, even before the symptoms arise.

✓ The changes in the Aura are created by changes in the attributes, and a proper knowledge of attributes is necessary to read and cleanse the Aura.

▶ The 23 Attributes:

There are three types of Guna (qualities). Their effects are explained in detail later.

1. Satwa
2. Rajas and
3. Tamas

There are five Tatwa (Elements in their subtle form). Their effects are explained in detail later.

4. Aakaash (Ether)
5. Vaayu (Air)
6. Tej (Fire or light)
7. Aap (Water or vapour) and
8. Prithvi (Earth or solid)

There are three types of Dosha (Impurities in their subtle form)

9. Vat means Gas. When Vat dominates, the person has problems with gas and stomach, and the effect of Vat on Aura is that of Vaayu, or Air element.

10. Pith means Acidity. When Pith dominates the person has problems with Acidity and anger, and the effect of Pith on Aura is that of Tej, or Fire element.

11. Cough means Cough. When Cough dominates, the person has problems with Cough and Cold and the effect of Kupph on Aura is that of Aap, or Water element. Most people are affected by these.

There are the seven Dhatu (Substances or metals in their subtle form)

12. Blood. This stands for the subtle form of energy responsible for the formation of blood. The substitute of blood is seen everywhere in nature, it is also seen as

balsam, resin, gum, milk, bdellium, benzoin, chicle etc. in the trees and plants.

13. Marrow. This stands for the subtle form of energy responsible for the formation of marrow. Like blood, the form of marrow is also seen in all forms of nature.

14. Skin. This stands for the subtle form of energy responsible for the formation of the outer protective layer in all forms of nature.

15. Flesh. This stands for the subtle form of energy responsible for the formation of the inner starchy or paddy layer in all forms of nature.

16. Sperms & Eggs. This stands for the subtle form of energy responsible for procreation in all forms of nature.

17. Bones. This stands for subtle form of energy responsible for the formation of inner hard structure in all forms of nature.

18. Virya. There is no appropriate word in English for Virya, it sounds somewhere near to the Sukra i.e. that is the sperms and eggs, but the meaning is very different and difficult to explain. And then there are,

19. Mind or intellect.

20. Memory

21. Awareness

22. Ego

23. Self or Soul.

This Universe and our Aura is made up of these twenty- three attributes and so are affected by them. How do these influence our thinking? Below are a few examples:

▶ Effects of the Three Guna

The Guna (Qualities), the Tatwa (Elements in their subtle form) and the Dosha (Impurities in their subtle form) dominate the Aura/mind the most and cast their effects, which become our second nature.

✓   When Satwa dominates then there is happiness, feeling of boredom, and sometimes things might seem unreal.

✓   When Rajas dominates then there is feverishness, anger, etc.

✓   When Tamas dominates then there is lethargy, untidiness, effect of black magic, jealousy etc.

▶ Effects of the Five Tatwa

The five Tatwas (Elements in their subtle form) are connected to the five sense organs and five work organs and have formed the five dimensions (in fact there are eleven dimensions connected to 5 sense organs, 5 work organs and the mind). Different Tatwa are dominant in different parts of the body. The five Tatwas along with the Dosha and the Guna also affect our Aura and in turns. Their effects are as follows:

✓   When Ether dominates, there is compassion, fear, love, discomfort or total comfort.

✓   When Air dominates, there is contentment, movement, need for change, escapism, greed, fear and hatred.

✓   When Fire dominates, there is truth, awareness, anger, and feverishness.

✓   When Water dominates, there is togetherness, lust, depression, floating, fear of being left out and forgiveness.

✓   When Earth dominates, there is consolidation, suicide tendency, heaviness, sincerity and ego.

It is important to note that no one Guna, Dosha or Tatwa can be dominant forever. They keep on changing with time. If it is observed that any one of the above dominates for more than two and a quarter day (i.e. the time taken by the Moon to shift from one constellation to another) then the person feels that attribute which is dominating for a long time is his or her true nature. For example, if Fire Element with Rajas Guna is dominant for a longer period, then the person starts feeling angry. To bring a shift one has to follow the five disciplines mentioned in the next section.

Tatwa	Sense Organ	Work Organ	Emotions	Dominated Body part
Earth	Nose	Anus	Consolidation, Suicidal tendency, Heaviness, Sincerity, Ego	Anus
Water	Tongue	Genitals	Togetherness, Lust, Depression, Floating, Fear of being left out, Forgiveness	Genitals
Air	Skin	Legs	Contentment, Lust, Movement, Need for change, Escapism, Greed, Fear, Hatred	Stomach and Heart
Fire	Eyes	Hands	Truth, Awareness, Anger, Feverishness	Third eye & Throat
Ether	Ear	Mouth	Compassion, Fear, Love, Discomfort, Comfort	Throat to head

SECTION 2

Disciplines to be observed to keep the Aura clean:

"Anything in life which has some value; needs patience, uninterrupted practice, respect and faith to be achieved."

'Hittesh Morjaria'

Everything in the Universe is moving. Movement is change, and if any one attribute dominates for a longer time then it causes sorrow, pain and boredom. There is a need to bring a shift, to circulate these attributes with help of five types of disciplines.

Thanks to Mother Nature that before a problem arises, there are five solutions raised, and before the illness five cures are suggested.

Likewise, if there is a problem with the Aura, five solutions are raised, which need to be practiced with dedication. These disciplines, if understood and adopted in the right manner, can make your life easy, comfortable and happy.

▶ **Food:**

What we eat or drink affects our Aura In our studies food is divided into three categories.

✓ Satwik food that allows Satwa to dominate - fresh fruits, raw vegetables etc.

✓ Rajsik food that allows Rajas to dominate - milk products, proteins, fat etc.

✓ Tamsik food which allows Tamas to dominate - spicy/ stale/ junk/ non-vegetarian food, alcohol, drugs etc.

    i.   Proper food balances our Aura. For example, if a person is short-tempered, s/he should avoid spices and drink more liquids to minimize the fire element with the help of water.

ii. The vessel in which you eat is also important as it also affects the Aura.

iii. Eating, drinking or cooking in a gold vessel increases vigor, light, power, awareness, lust, anger, ego etc.

iv. Eating, drinking or cooking in a silver vessel increases calmness, beauty, creativity, eyesight, laziness, boredom etc.

v. Eating, drinking or cooking in a glass vessel increases fear, comfort, discomfort, poverty, dullness etc.

vi. Eating, drinking or cooking in a steel vessel increases anger, awareness, strength etc.

vii. Eating, drinking or cooking in a clay vessel increases awareness, calmness, patience, compassion, truthfulness, boredom, laziness etc.

viii. Eating, drinking or cooking in an aluminum vessel increases negativity, bodily illness, mental fatigue, restlessness, fear etc.

ix. Eating, drinking or cooking in a copper vessel increases fearlessness, good health, vigor, tidiness, upset stomach, anger etc.

x. Eating, drinking or cooking in a brass vessel increases power, ego etc.

xi. Eating, drinking or cooking in a plastic vessel increases negativity, illness, mental fatigue, sorrow, fear etc.

xii. The direction we face while eating or drinking is also very important. Eating or drinking facing the south is very harmful as it causes illness and the Aura absorbs a lot of negativity.

xiii. Eating or not eating at different hours also creates negativity. Never eat after midnight to dawn and always eat something after dawn before noon.

xiv. Nature is very intelligent. It grows specially required food in the place and time where and when it is needed. It is always healthy for your body and your Aura.

xv. Water is the most powerful purifier. It must run through the body in and out. As you bathe to keep your outer body clean, the same way we should drink a lot of water to keep the body clean from inside.

xvi. There are two types of foods---solid and liquid-- that we intake and the other is the thoughts. That's the reason you must have good thoughts and be in positive surroundings to attract good thoughts. People wanting to practice Aura cleansing for others must meditate so that they don't absorb negativity and transfer negativity to their subject.

▶ Rest:

When you rest your Aura expands and absorbs energy from the surrounding, but excessive rest might also absorb negativity or drain energy.

✓ Eight hours sleep is necessary for an average person. But if the person is high on awareness or is practicing meditation or chanting, then he can do with less hours of sleep.

✓ The time that we sleep is also important. Sleeping at odd hours will collect negativity. The perfect time for sleeping is at night and the perfect time for a nap is in the afternoon when the sun is over the head.

✓ It is very harmful to sleep during dusk.

✓ It is very helpful to be awake at dawn.

✓ Direction in which we sleep is also very important. All the vibrations of the earth travel towards the North, so sleeping with the head facing the North will cause illness and fatigue.

Only dead bodies must be kept that way as it helps to release all energy, which is in the form of thoughts and desire, faster.

✓ A person who sleeps on his right side torso is naturally happy. One who sleeps on his left side recovers faster from illness but one must only sleep towards his left side if he or she is unwell or has a habit of sleeping immediately after having his or her meal. A person sleeping on his stomach is full of desire and lust. A person sleeping on his back is a perfect yogi he can heal people and is always naturally healthy. It is important that you listen to your body and sleep accordingly. In a normal state, it is advisable to sleep on our back and during illness it is advisable to sleep on your left side for quick recovery. People planning to learn Aura cleansing must learn the art of sleeping in the direction necessary for them. Sleeping on the back is the position recommended for them.

▶ **Time:**

You will see that all these five principles are inter-connected. The time factor is mentioned in all the principles. There are four aspects of time that affect the Aura, which are:

i.   The era in which we are living i.e. the 'Kaliyuga' the black era.

ii. The time of the day.

iii. The planetary effects on an individual at the present time.

iv. Season.

✓ As per the Hindu scriptures, we live in the dark era (Kalyuga). In this era, the negative effectsare more than the positive ones. The most powerful thing is the name i.e. chanting. Through chanting, a person can remove a lot of negativity, attract a lot of positive vibes and bliss, and also attain salvation. People doing regular chanting carry a healthy Aura. The use of proper mantra is also necessary for the process of Aura cleansing to succeed.

✓ From 12 to 3 in the afternoon and at night is the time when negativity energy is at its peak. Doing any thing good, like eating, Aura cleansing, meditating at that time is not advisable. However during this time period some special occult rituals of Aura cleansing for a person severely affected by black magic are carried out.

✓ **Rahukaal:** Each day has a time period which is considered inauspicious for starting something new, to meditate or do Aura cleansing. Experts performing Aura cleansing during Rahukaal will not only absorb negativity from the patient's, Aura, but will also fail to cleanse the Aura completely.

✓ To know the Rahukaal better, first lets know about the Mohurat. One Mohurat is of a duration of one and a half hours. There are eight Mohurats in the day time and eight at night. So 1.5 multiplied by 16 Mouhrats (8 of day plus 8 of night) of a day gives us 24 hours.

✓ The time of the first Mohurat of the day starts with sun rise. Time of the last Mohurat of the day ends at the time of sunrise of the next day, which also marks the first Mohurat of that day.

✓ For example: if I want to check all the Mohurats of Sunday in Mumbai, where the approximate time of sunrise is 6:30 am, then the time of all sixteen Mohurats of the sunday will be as under:

- 1st Mohurat starts from 6:30 am and ends at 8:00 am on Sunday.
- 2nd Mohurat starts from 8:00 am and ends at 9:30 am on Sunday.
- 3rd Mohurat starts from 9:30 am and ends at 11:00 am on Sunday.
- 4th Mohurat starts from 11:00 am and ends at 12:30 pm on Sunday.

- 5th Mohurat starts from 12:30 pm and ends at 2:00 pm on Sunday.
- 6th Mohurat starts from 2:00 pm and ends at 3:30 pm on Sunday.
- 7th Mohurat starts from 3:30 pm and ends at 5:00 pm on Sunday.
- 8th Mohurat starts from 5:00 pm and ends at 6:30 pm on Sunday.

The 8 Mohurats starts and ends from 6:30 am to 6:30 pm on a Sunday. Then starts the night Mohurat.

- 1st Mohurat starts from 6:30 pm and ends at 8:00 pm on Sunday.
- 2nd Mohurat starts from 8:00 pm and ends at 9:30 pm on Sunday.
- 3rd Mohurat starts from 9:30 pm and ends at 11:00 pm on Sunday.
- 4th Mohurat starts from 11:00 pm Sunday and ends at 12:30 am on Monday. (The Hindu time system of the day start and end differs from the western system of 12:00 am to 12:00 am. As per the Hindu system the day starts at sunrise and ends at sunrise the next day)
- 5th Mohurat starts from 12:30 am and ends at 2:00 am on Monday.
- 6th Mohurat starts from 2:00 am and ends at 3:30 am on Monday.
- 7th Mohurat starts from 3:30 am and ends at 5:00 am on Monday.
- 8th Mohurat starts from 5:00 am and ends at 6:30 am on Monday.
- The first Mohurat of Monday will start from 6:30 am on Monday.

This is an example to simplify the understanding of the Mohurats. If the dawn breaks at 7:00 am or 7:30 am in winter or as per your country timings, then calculate the first Mohurat from that time.

There are seven types of effects of the Mohurats all together (called Chougadia). Out of these three are auspicious, one is neutral and three are inauspicious for starting something new. They are as follows:

1. Shubh means auspicious. It is a good Mohurat to start anything new. It is said that new start ups during this time proves to be lucky.

2. Laabh means beneficial. It is a good Mohurat to start something auspicious. It is said that anything started in this time will turn out to be very beneficial.

3. Amrit means immortal. It is a good Mohurat. It is said that anything started at this time will sustain for long.

4. Chal means average. It is an okay Mohurat. It is said that anything started at this time will turn out to be just fine.

5. Kaal means death. It is a bad Mohurat to start something auspicious. It is said that anything started at this time will cause deadly consciences, or will not sustain for long.

6. Rog means disease. It is a bad Mohurat to start something auspicious. It is said that anything started in this time will bring in bad health.

7. Udhveg which means restlessness. It is a bad Mohurat. It is said that anything started in this time will cause fights.

There is a special effect on Mohurats called the Rahukaal, which falls along with any one of the above Mohurats which creates hurdles. It is not advisable to perform Aura cleansing on someone or start something new or meditate during Rahukaal. (Refer to the chart above for more clarification).

Sun	Mon	Tues	Wed	Thurs	Fri	Sat
Udhveg	Amrit	Rog	Laabh	Shubh	Chal	Kaal
Chal	Kaal RahuKal	Udhveg	Amrit	Rog	Laabh	Shubh
Laabh	Shubh	Chal	Kaal	Udhveg	Amrit	Rog RahuKal
Amrit	Rog	Laabh	Shubh	Chal	Kaal RahuKal	Udhveg
Kaal	Udhveg	Amrit	Rog RahuKal	Laabh	Shubh	Chal
Shubh	Chal	Kaal	Udhveg	Amrit RahuKal	Rog	Laabh
Rog	Laabh	Shubh RahuKal	Chal	Kaal	Udhveg	Amrit
Udhveg RahuKal	Amrit	Rog	Laabh	Shubh	Chal	Kaal

Please check the chart below for the different Mohurats of the night.

Sun	Mon	Tues	Wed	Thurs	Fri	Sat
Shubh	Chal	Kaal	Udhveg	Amrit	Rog	Laabh
Amrit	Rog	Laabh	Shubh	Chal	Kaal	Udhveg
Chal	Kaal	Udhveg	Amrit	Rog	Laabh	Shubh
Rog	Laabh	Shubh	Chal	Kaal	Udhveg	Amrit
Kaal	Udhveg	Amrit	Rog	Laabh	Shubh	Chal
Laabh	Shubh	Chal	Kaal	Udhveg	Amrit	Rog
Udhveg	Amrit	Rog	Laabh	Shubh	Chal	Kaal
Shubh	Chal	Kaal	Udhveg	Amrit	Rog	Laabh

People who don't understand can leave this complicated time pattern of auspicious and inauspicious, just praying to your mentor (Guru) helps remove all kinds of obstacles, in auspiciousness and negativity.

▶ **Environment:**

The environment affects us and vice versa.

✓ Friends, relatives and the company of people we keep. It is also observed that couples who are in deep love for a long time start looking and thinking like each other. People who have pets also start looking like their pets. Love and hatred are the strongest emotions and the people we love or hate affect our Aura the most. (Also those we are surrounded by).

✓ Cleanliness of our surroundings i.e. our house, work place and our body is important. Among the elements water is the best cleanser, it runs well through our body, both on the inside and outside. Daily bath and drinking a lot of water is useful. Drinking more water in the day time is helpful but drinking excess water after sunset is not good. Using Aura cleansing salts for bathing and mopping helps even more. The Aura of our room can be cleansed by burning Aura cleansing lemon incenses sticks and once in a while performing havan. Chanting loudly or playing soft and soothing Aura cleansing **'Meditation Sounds'** in a room cleanses it off the negative energies. Chanting in the mind cleanses our Aura too. Sounds of fights, abuses, screams and crying even if it is coming from the television or any musical instrument spoils the Aura of the room.

✓ The part of the world where we live is also very important; the climate also affects the Aura. Fresh air, height, moisture, heat, cold everything affects our Aura. Usage of air-conditioning for a long time is very bad for the Aura.

✓ Things we wear-colour, material and fitting of our clothes, makeup, stones, Rudraksh everything affects our Aura. We will see in the further chapters the detail about how these affect our mind and in turn the Aura.

▶ **Love or Attention:**

This is the most powerful aspect among all others. There are many aspects of love or attention like meditation, Aura cleansing, being in love or **loving yourself.**

✓ It has been seen that people who are in love generally glow. This is because love makes the Aura powerful and bright, it has also been seen that after Aura cleansing or meditation a person looks brighter.

✓ In the later chapters, we will discuss in details about Aura cleansing. There are **training sessions** to train people to become expert Aura cleaners.

✓ There are CDs available for cleansing your Aura and Chakra, and making it strong and powerful to restrain all types of negativity.

SECTION
3

Degrees of Aura:

"Everything of this world can be measured,
so the Hindu's have called this world as Maya,
Maya means that which can be measured or which is illusion.
That which can't be measured is divine, for example, love.
Love is divine without boundaries or perfection limits.
Love is not an illusion but it creates an illusion."

'Hittesh Morjaria'

Like everything in this worlds, Aura can be measured too.

Aura has different layers, yet connected as one. There are units (called Ungal or Kalaa in Sanskrit) of Prana in everything that is seen and the size of Aura also depends on the number of units the object has.

- ✓ All non-living things, plants and gross things made of earth element have one unit (Ungal or Kalaa) of Prana.

- ✓ All living beings in water like fishes and water element have two units (Ungal or Kalaa) of Prana.

- ✓ All living beings holding fire and fire element have three units (Ungal or Kalaa) of Prana.

- ✓ All aerial living beings and air element have four units (Ungal or Kalaa) of Prana.

- ✓ All ether or space elements have five units (Ungal or Kalaa) of Prana. The more subtle the element, the more units of Prana it can hold.

- ✓ Animals have five units (Ungal or Kalaa) of Prana.

- ✓ Humans have more than six units (Ungal or Kalaa) of Prana that is around six inches.

✓ It is said that if the size of Aura of a human goes below six units or if the last thought at the time of death of a human being is of an animal, (which is possible as a result of too much attachment with an animal or if a person is being killed by the animal). In that case, the human is reborn as an animal or else gets enlightened.

✓ Like the elements, the more subtle in nature a human or a living being is, the more units of Prana or we can say a bigger Aura he or she can hold.

✓ A human being who has all his Chakra active and has an Aura of minimum ten units, i.e. approximately ten inches or more, will have a chance to be liberated in this life time.

✓ A human Aura can go up to fifteen units, not more than that, rarely you would find a person who is an enlightened incarnation and his or her's Aura/Prana. Sixteen units which is the highest.

✓ It has been said in the ancient scriptures that only incarnation of Goddess Kali or Lord Krishna, who were the complete incarnation of the creator, sustainer and destroyer had an Aura of sixteen units.

✓ There is one more interesting research that Lord Hanuman, who served Lord Ram, had more units of Aura than Lord Ram as he always had an attitude of service in his mind.

Prashnop Upanishad

Question six asked by Sukesha to the enlightened sage Pipalaacharia about the complete Purush (God almighty), the creator, sustainer and destroyer of the universe, the one who has sixteen Kala or units of Aura/Prana, which means one who is matured in all aspects of life.

After that Sukesha the son of Bhardhwraj asked Pipaladaacharia "O enlightened God! The prince of Kaushal 'Hiraniyanabh came to me and asked this question, O son of Bhardhwraj, do you know the Purush who has sixteen Kala (units of Aura)? To this, I responded to the prince that I do not know him. Why would I not tell you, if I would have known him; a person who speaks ambiguously without knowledge gets dried from all directions including from his source; hence I cannot speak without knowledge. Getting this answer, he left quietly on his chariot. So I pray to tell me who and where is the great saint?

On this, Pipaladaacharia answered, "O Somya (the beautiful one) the one in whom these sixteen units are glimpsed that Purush is residing in this body !2!

Main Components of Aura

"One of the root cause of misery is fear of the unknown;
we remain confined in the known, and so life becomes a repetition,
a circle. Because of this continuous repetitive routine life, one feels
misery, boredom, futility. Life is tremendously beautiful,
but we never go into the unknown and life belongs to the unknown.
The more alive you become, then life has newness, youth.
Nothing is repeated, hence no boredom is created.
Every morning brings something new, unexpected, uninvited"

'Osho'

▶ Chakra:

There are thousands of energy circulation points formed in a human body called the Chakra. According to yoga, there are seven major energy circles, which create strong impulses of different kinds on the Aura / mind, and allow the energy to move upwards or downwards. The placement and the functions of different Chakra are as follows.

i.   The Mulaadhar Chakra located at the base of the spine, it is also called the base Chakra or root Chakra. It is situated at the base of the spine where the anus is. When it is active then creativity, suicidal tendencies, stiffness or excitement is experienced. The name Mulaadhar means root support. The colour of Mulaadhar Chakra is red, in a holistic healthy person (a person who is mentally, spiritually and physically fit).

    a.   Many Reki schools and western clairvoyants consider the Mulaadhar Chakra and Swadhisthan Chakra as one, as they are very small and very near to each other.

b. It is seen that the artists all over the world are caught up in sex scandals, but some artistic people especially painters are so involved in their art that they are unaware of sex completely.

c. It is strange but true that most homosexuals and bisexuals are also artistic people. Either they are too much into sex or they are totally off it.

ii. The Swadhisthan Chakra is located behind the genitals, is also called the sex Chakra. When it is active then sharing, showing off, lust or depression is experienced. The name Swadhisthan means the land of taste. The colour of Swadhisthan Chakra is orange in a holistic healthy person.

a. When the energy flows downwards from Swadhisthan to Mulaadhar then depression leads to suicidal tendencies and when the energy flows upwards from Mulaadhar to Swadhisthan then art and creativity leads to sharing.

iii. The Manipur Chakra is located behind the Navel, is also called the stomach Chakra. When it is active, then generosity, satisfaction, greed or jealousy is experienced. The name Manipur means the town of jewels. It is here where our past life Karma is stored. The colour of Manipur Chakra is yellow in a holistic healthy person.

a. Generosity is the one most obviously connected to the stomach in all the religions. All generously giving saints and gods like the Laughing Buddha, Ganesha, Santa Claus have big bellies.

iv. The Anaahat Chakra is located in-between the two nipples, it is also called the heart Chakra. When it is active then love, fear or hatred is experienced. The name Anaahat means the un-struck sound. The colour of Anaahat Chakra is green in a holistic healthy person.

a. A person feels butterflies in the heart or touches the heart when he or she is experiencing love, hatred or fear. All these three are the most powerful human emotions.

v. The Vishuddhi Chakra is located in the throat, is also called the throat Chakra. When it is active then gratitude, sorrow or guilt is experienced. The name Vishuddhi means the purifier of poisons. The colour of Vishuddhi Chakra is blue in a holistic healthy person; here the poisons entering the body via food are first purified.

a. Lord Shiva drank the poison called Harahar for the planet to survive, and stored it in his throat; his throat turned blue for which he is known as 'NeelKanth' which means one with a blue throat. The way I interpret this is that our criticism of people must come only from the throat, it must not come from the heart or the head because if it comes from the heart or the head it will harm us or the person we are criticizing or both. But if it is only from the throat then the person will change for the better.

vi. The Aangya Chakra is located in-between the two eyebrows where the third eye is situated, it is also called the third-eye Chakra. When it is active, then awareness, knowledge or anger is experienced. The name Aangya means orders. The color of Aangya Chakra in a holistic healthy person is Indigo.

a. By means of this Chakra the person can be given suggestions or orders to let go of some habit or to follow some discipline. This is the point of hypnotism.

b. Intuitions of people having Aangya chakra more active are very strong, but it is also seen that people who are not channeling the energy properly will only get negative intuitions of the future, and they will also not be able to distinguish between intuitions and their cravings and desires.

c.　It is also seen that people having strong awareness or urge for perfection will lose their temper very fast. This is a sign of Aangya Chakra being over active. So it is seen that want of perfection is the cause of all anger and trouble in the world.

vii.　The Sahastrar is located on the Crown, it is also called the Crown Chakra. Most of the schools of Yoga do not consider it as a Chakra since there is no negative or positive feelings here, but when it is active, then only bliss is experienced, which is free of good or bad or negative or positive. The color of Sahastrar in a holistic healthy person is Violet.

a.　The name Sahastrar means thousand petals.

b.　If the energy traveling via the spine called the Kundalini Shakti reaches this Chakra the person is free from all negativity as well as positivity and is blissful and pure.

i.　It is important to know that 'no' two impulses of the same Chakra can arise at the same time. Love, hatred and fear are of the Anaahat Chakra and a person experiencing love can never feel hatred or fear.

ii.　The effects of downward and upward flow of energy called Kundalini from these Chakras will be explained in the next chapter.

iii.　I have included a meditation to activate, cleanse and enhance all your Chakras in a meditation compact disc given with this book.

iv. As per one of the schools of Indian occult (Tantra) there are three more chakras other than what Yoga mentions. They are all placed between the third eye (Aangya) Chakra and the Crown (Sahastrar), placed one above the other touching each other and leaving no room for any space in between the third eye and the crown. They are as under:

    a.   Lalaat

    b.   Golat

    c.   Trilat

✓ These Chakras need to be given attention or cleansed only in cases of 'Blue stars'. The phrase 'Blue stars' means people who hallucinate, feel they are speaking to God or the dead. I do not disagree with the powers of clairvoyants as I am one of them, but I do not agree to people who say they talk to God or see God. You can have vision of or communicate with Fairies or Angles whom the Hindus call deities but you cannot see God as you are God and everything is God.

✓ Out of all the people claiming themselves to be clairvoyants only a few are found to be genuine, the rest are either fakes or 'Blue stars'.

✓ Fake clairvoyants are people who lie to the world about their psychic abilities but 'Blue stars' are people who lie to themselves, it would not be wrong if I said that they are fools who steal from their own pockets.

✓ There is a very thin line between the real clairvoyant and a 'Blue star', which needs to be watched carefully. My observation says that training in this field without a proper Guru will lead one to the state of a 'Blue star'.

✓ As per one of the schools of Reiki, there is one more important Chakra than what Yoga mentions. It is the Solar plexus

Chakra located at the solar plexus, which is very important to be cleansed in artistic, over emotional people and women (the Anahat Chakra being situated in between the nipples, is at the solar plex for women).

✓ These Chakras are governed by different Tatwa (Elements) i.e. the Mulaadhar or the base Chakra which is governed by the earth element. But more on that later in this book.

▶ The Hand Chakra:

There are very important Chakras after the above mentioned Chakras in both our palms. They are known as the left palm chakra, the right palm Chakra and the finger tips Chakras. It is very important for a professional Aura cleanser to know these Chakras.

✓ The left palm Chakra is situated in the center of the left palm.

✓ The right palm Chakra is situated in the center of the right palm.

✓ These palm Chakras are responsible for the exchange of our body energy with the energies of others when we shake hands, touch feet, hug or join hands in namaskar.

✓ The size of this Chakras vary from one to two inches in diameter. The bigger Chakras indicates that the the person will be a better healer, and the more a person practices meditation and does more Aura cleansing, these Chakras will increase in size.

✓ The right handed people release energy (Prana) from the right hand and absorb energy from the left hand and the left handed people release energy (Prana) from the left hand and absorb energy from the right hand.

✓ So a right handed person must do Aura cleansing with the right hand keeping the left hand open towards the sky to absorb energy and a left handed person must do Aura cleansing with the left hand keeping the right hand open towards the sky.

✓ There are ten small chakras on your ten finger tips. Their functions are as under.

    i.   The function of the little finger is to warn oneself.

    ii.   The function of the ring finger is for spirituality.

    iii.   The function of the middle finger is for medication.

    iv.   The function of the index finger is to warn or stop others.

    v.   The function of the thumb is to cheer or boost up others.

    h.   In our Meditation Compact Disc, we have included an exercise which will activate these Chakras.

    i.   It is very important for a professional Aura cleanser to activate these twelve Chakras.

► Technique to enhance the power and size of hands and finger Chakras:

There is a very ancient technique called the Kar Nayas, to enhance the power of the palm and finger Chakras. Kar Nayas is practiced before performing any kind of ritual with the hands. The process is very easy, and by experience I have found out that this technique which is generally practiced with Sanskrit Mantras is equally effective if done with complete attention and faith without the Sanskrit sholkas. The Kar Nayas technique is given below:

✓ Sit comfortably and easily with your spine erect, head straight, shoulders relaxed and a smile on your face.

✓ Keep your palms facing the ceiling and pinch the center of your palms with the nails of your middle fingers, so attention remains in the center of your palms.

✓ Make loose fists with both your palms.

✓ Take deep breaths and concentrate totally on both your palms.

✓ Slowly shift your attention to the tips of both your thumbs and open them with total awareness.

✓ Slowly shift your attention to the tips of both your index fingers and open them with total awareness.

✓ Slowly shift your attention to the tips of both your middle fingers and open them with total awareness.

✓ Slowly shift your attention to the tips of both your ring fingers and open them with total awareness.

✓ Slowly shift your attention to the tips of both your little fingers and open them with total awareness.

✓ Now that both your palms are open bring your attention to the center of your left palm and slap it with the middle and index finger of your right hand curling back the other fingers.

✓ Open your right palm again and bring your attention to the center of your right palm and slap it with the middle and index finger of your left hand bending back your other fingers.

✓ Keep both your palms facing the ceiling and bring your attention to both palms and you will feel the palm and finger Chakras of both your palms activated and rotating.

▶ Kundalini:

Kundalini means ring. There is a coiled energy at the base of our spine at the Mulaadhar Chakra. It is coiled in three and a half rounds like a snake, so it is called the Kundalini Shakti which means 'coiled energy.'

✓ It makes an upwards movement with the help of the clocks wise movements of our seven main chakras.

✓ In the same way it crawls downwards with the anti clockwise movements of Chakras.

✓ The Kundalini Shakti is red in colour and its nature is that of Tej or Fire element. So it is said that the upwards movement is its nature like the nature of fire is to move upwards.

✓ The upwards movement of the Kundalini makes a being intelligent and blissful.

✓ The downwards movement of the Kundalini makes a being lethargic, foolish and depressed.

✓ The easiest movement for Kundalini, as per her nature is to move upwards in a straight vertical direction.

✓ Human beings are the only species among living beings who have their spine erect in a straight vertical position, have the Kundalini more activated than any other living being, and so are, the most intelligent and developed than any other living being on this planet.

✓ As per its nature, it is easy for a Kundalini to travel upwards than downwards.

✓ But somehow most of the human beings are so surrounded by stress that the upwards movement is rarely observed.

✓ People who maintain a good posture are naturally blissful and intelligent.

◆ The Downward flow of Kundalini:

If the person is blissful, all he needs is a little anger that makes his eyebrows twitch and pulls him down. So from Sahastrar, the energy comes down to Aangya Chakra. After anger, the person feels a choke of guilt in the neck. So from Aangya Chakra, the energy comes down to Vishuddhi Chakra. If the guilt increases, then it turns into hatred or fear of the heart. So from Vishuddhi Chakra the energy comes down to Anaahat Chakra. If hatred or fear is not attended to, then it creates a burning sensation of greed or jealousy in the stomach. So from Anaahat Chakra, the energy comes down to Manipur Chakra. That brings the depression lower so from Manipur Chakra, the energy comes down to Swadhisthan Chakra. That finally leads to the suicidal tendency and the person feels there is nothing left in this world, he has hit the rock bottom, so from Swadhisthan Chakra the energy comes down to Mulaadhar Chakra.

◆ The Upward flow of Kundalini :

If the person is totally negative towards life and has suicidal thoughts in his mind, then a slight change towards creativity will help him to shift his focus. Here the Mulaadhar Chakra starts generating positive energy instead of negativity. After the creative work, the person feels like sharing or exhibiting his creation, so the energy has moved upwards from Mulaadhar Chakra to Swadhisthan Chakra. After exhibition comes the time to share it with people, so generosity moves the Kundalini Shakti to the navel or Manipur Chakra from Swadhisthan Chakra. Generosity always gives way to love which rises energy from the Manipur Chakra to the Anaahat Chakra. Love brings a lot of gratefulness, transporting the Kundalini Shakti to the Vishuddhi Chakra. A grateful person is full of awareness of the aid and help received from the world and that sends the energy to the higher plane of Aangya Chakra from the Vishuddhi Chakra. Awareness if sustained will bring the person back to his or her original nature that is bliss and the energy is at its peak at the Sahastrar.

Look at the chart below for a quick reference.

Chakra	Upward Emotion	Downward Emotion
Sahastrar	Bliss	-
Aangya	Awareness, knowledge	Anger
Vishuddhi	Gratefulness	Guilt or Sorrow
Anaahat	Love	Hatred or Fear
Manipur	Generosity, satisfaction	Greed or Jealousy
Swadhisthan	Sharing	Depression or lust
Mulaadhar	creativity or excitement	Suicidal tendency or stiffness

Seeing the Aura

"Those who have eyes will see"

'Jesus Christ'

▶ Basics of Seeing the Aura

Seeing the Aura is an easy task for people who believe in it and difficult task for those who do not believe. There are three types of beliefs needed to learn something

i.   Believing in your self, knowing you can and will see an Aura.

ii.   Believing in the technique. There are many techniques, but if you get stuck in choices then it will be difficult. Know that the technique you are following, which is in your hands right now, is the best.

iii.   Believing in the master who is training you.

✓   If you doubt any one of the above, the doubt for the other two will follow. It is the best to doubt the doubt as soon as it arises, and this is the best way to remove it.

✓   The second thing necessary after the faith is patience, as without patience you will reach nowhere.

✓   When everyone including the children can see the Aura by little practice, this means two things:

i.   Aura exists, and people seeing it are neither hallucinating nor lying.

ii.   Seeing the Aura is a natural process and can be developed by every human being.

▶ How did I start seeing the Aura?

*"Infinite emptiness will be mirrored. Two mirrors facing each other.
But if you have any idea, then you will see your own idea in me."*

'Osho'

✓ When I was in my teens, I would buy books on meditation with the little pocket money I saved, from an old books dealer. I brought an old magazine one day in which it was mentioned that by doing Agani Tratak (fire gazing) for fifty two days one can start seeing Auras.

✓ The method was mentioned inside. All I had to do is gaze at a burning incense stick kept ten feet away. There was also a method of Pranayam mentioned as it is dangerous to do Tratak without knowing Pranayam.

✓ Followed that process, since in the past I had benefited from a certain type of meditation mentioned in that particular organization's magazine.

✓ I did that particular meditation for six days and I could see a white cloud floating in my room. I tried to figure what it was? For a moment, I confess, I though I felt a presence in the room. I figured out that this might be a spirit as it started floating towards me. Since I was completly naked as per the instructions of the magazine and the spirit was near my clothes, I pulled a bed sheet around me and ran out of the room.

✓ I was so scared that, I stopped doing that meditation and was afraid to enter my own room.

✓ One thing was for sure that I started seeing spirits but could not see the Aura. It was like buying a ticket to fly to London reaching Tokyo instead.

✓ After a while, I started doing the same meditation as I was determined to see the Aura, but even after continuous efforts, I could not see the Aura and so I lost patience. I overdid the

Agani Tratak. I would request my brother, sister and friends to volunteer and sit in a dark room in front of me so I could see their Aura. Fed up of this, I started getting restless after each failed attempt.

✓ Finally after several trial and error, dropped the idea.

✓ After a few years when on I travelled to small villages of the two states, Maharashtra and Karnataka, due to my grandfather's business, in which we had to visit sugar factories located there.

✓ There were many unknown sadhus (Hindu saints) in the small villages, who had some type of special powers or great wisdom, so I made it a point to learn something from any sadhu I met.

✓ Sometimes this type of enthusiasm became dangerous for me, and only by the grace of God I survived and continued my quest.

✓ One day I had to visit a small village called Mangalweda near Pandharpur (which is one of the biggest pilgrimage places in Maharashtra). I had to visit a factory near to Mangalweda. After my visit, I came back to Mangalweda to proceed back to Pandharpur and from there to Sangli where my grandfather had his base.

✓ I had some time in hand, so I visited a small temple built near the bus stand in which I had to crawl inside. There I saw a sadhu sitting inside doing Agani Tratak on Scared seeing each other, I rushed out and then gathered my self and waited for him. Within a few seconds, even he was out with his blanket perched on his shoulder.

✓ I touched his feet to show respect and asked his name, he blessed me and said his name was Ramaanand, I asked him why was he practising Agani Tratak? He never bothered to answer. His disinterested aroused my curiosity. So I confessed,

'I have done this for quiet a while just to see Aura but I do not think it helped in any way'.

✓ He thought for a moment and said, 'it is not necessary to do Agani Tratak to see Aura, you can see Aura without it, it is not that difficult' I began pleading him to teach me the technique to see Aura. He was reluctant at first, but given my persistence threw an offer to put me off. He said 'you will have to pay me all the money you have right now in your pocket'.

✓ I was taken aback, but thought for a while that he is saying this only to put me off and I knew that these sadhu only give knowledge to those deserving after testing him. Also, I was not very sure after so many failures, whether he will be able to teach me, but I agreed and followed him inside the cave and into the same temple.

✓ Within fifteen minutes, I could see the Aura of the Sadhu and the idols. Once out of the place, I could see the Aura of the temple, trees, people, of everyone and everything around. I was very pleased and he blessed me saying that I will be able to teach this technique to others who will believe in it too.

✓ Then he demanded his fees, I promptly agreed to give him all the money I had except for the hundred rupees as that was the approximate bus fare I needed to reach Sangli. He became angry and asked me to pay all the money I had. So without bargaining I gave him all the money I had.

✓ I walked to the Purchase officer's house which was nearby and borrowed the money to return to Sangli.

✓ I later could teach many of my students to see the Aura the way I could, and here I am going to share this technique with you.

✓ Throughout the years, I have also noticed that one can easily see an Aura through a video or the camera of your mobile phones. The Aura is very easily and clearly visible if the person is shot from a distance with a white background.

▶ Techniques to see the Aura with naked eyes:

"O Lord let my ears hear Auspicious words,
let my eyes see Auspicious sights,
with a still body let me Pray to you for a long life
Aum Peace ! Peace ! Peace !!"

'Mandukyuopanishad'

▶ Pranayam:

For any kind of meditation, it is necessary to follow some do's and don'ts. Pranayam means breathing exercise. It also means controlling or formatting the vital breath.

    i.   The technique of Pranayam used to see Aura is called Nadi Shodhan Pranayam. It has other benefits too. It helps activate both the sides of your brain, and enhances one's intuitions, etc.

• Nadi Shodhan Pranayam Technique is as under:

✓ Keep your back straight, in line with your head, eyes closed and shoulders relaxed; keep a smile on your face and drop your body weight on the ground that you are sitting on. Be sure that you are not crossing your hands or legs unless you are sitting crossed legs in Sukh-Asana (cross legged posture), or Padma-Asana (lotus posture).

✓ Keep your right hands thumb on the right nostril, your index and middle finger in between the eyebrows where your third eye is and your ring and little finger on the left nostril.

✓ Your left hand must be on your left lap facing the ceiling in Chin Mudra i.e. the index finger lightly touching the thumb.

✓ Breathe out through both your nostrils pushing your stomach in. Remember that whenever you breath in, your stomach comes out and whenever you breath out your stomach will go in. This is a thumb rule.

✓ For the first round, block your right nostril by pressing it with your right hand thumb and very slowly breathe in through your left nostril.

✓ Then block your left nostril by pressing it with your right hand ring and little finger and very slowly breathe out through your right nostril, releasing the right hand thumb in the process.

✓ After breathing out completely, keep your left nostril blocked by pressing it with your right hand ring and little finger and very slowly breathe in through your right nostril.

✓ Then block your right nostril by pressing it with your right hand thumb and very slowly breathe out through your left nostril, releasing it by loosening your ring and little finger. So, breathing in from your left nostril and breathing out from your right nostril, then breathing in again from your right nostril and breathing out from your left nostril. This completes one full round of Nadi Shodhan Pranayam.

✓ Follow this pattern for nine rounds, breathing very slowly. Completing this should take you at least take five minutes.

✓ After completing nine rounds, wait for two minutes, sitting quietly and observing your breathing pattern. Slowly you will become aware of the surroundings. Take a while to open your eyes and start chanting Aum.

This is the best Pranayam for beginners learning any art of divination or wanting any kind of Siddhi (supernatural powers).

Siddhi is also called Apashu Shakti means power, which is beyond the control of any living being (even humans); a power, which does not want to control or destroy, a power, which is non-violent; and a power, which is also called love or innocence.

▶ Chanting the Pranav :

There are three natural sounds in the Universe. They are AA, OU, and MM.

✓ If you see any person of any religion, cast or colour; in any part of the world, they will only cry out in these three sounds when in pain, emotionally or physically. The best thing is no one has taught us to do so, these sounds come out naturally.

✓ It is amazing that all the religions of the world have combined these three sounds called the Pranav, by the Hindus, to form a spiritual sound. Like the Hindus, Jains, Buddhists, Sikhs and Chinese pronounce it as "AUM"; the Christians spell it as "AMEN"; the Muslims and Parsi's say it as "AAMIN"; the Jews as "SHALLAUM" and so on.

✓ These sounds represent the trinity of God head; AA represents the Creator or the father and the vibrations of AA are felt in the stomach region where all the reproductive and creative organs like stomach and genitals are placed, OU represents the Sustainer or the son and the vibrations of OU are felt in the heart region where all the sustaining and nourishing organs like heart, lungs and ribs are placed. MM represents the Destroyer or the holy spirit and the vibrations of MM are felt in the head region where the brain is.

✓ Like with the Pranayam, the chanting of Pranav in odd numbers of times is also important.

Please note that it is not advisable to chant any of the Pranav i.e. AUM, AAMIN, AMEN etc. in even number of times.

▶ Chanting the Pranav technique is as under:

✓ Keep your back straight, in line with the head, eyes closed and shoulders relaxed; keep a smile on your face and drop your body weight to the ground that you are sitting on.

✓ Your hands must be on your lap facing the ceiling, in Chin Mudra i.e. the index finger lightly touching the thumb.

✓ Ensure your hands and legs are not in crossed position, unless you are sitting in Sukh-Asana (cross legged posture), or Padma-Asana (lotus posture).

✓ Take three deep breaths. Remember, whenever you breath in your stomach will come out and whenever you breath out, your stomach will go in. This is a thumb rule.

✓ Take a deep breath and chant AUM or any form of Pranav you like. Breathe out and slowly start chanting the long Pranav, in a way that it vibrates your whole being.

✓ Take another deep breath in and breathing out you start chanting the long Pranav in a way that it vibrates your whole being.

✓ Breathr in and breathe once before you start chanting the long Pranav in a way that it vibrates your whole being

Remember Pranav must not be chanted in even numbers, but in odd numbers. To release the right kind of energies in your system.

▶ **The first technique to see the Aura taught to me by the Sadhu in Mangalweda :**

✓ After doing your Pranayam and chanting Pranav for three times, sit comfortably and easily in a dimly room with a white wall or a background.

✓ Get a volunteer to sit still in front of you at a distance of seven to ten feet, approximately two to three meters. Make sure s/he has a white background behind him or her.

✓ Open both your palms and bring them four inches closer to each other, keeping little a distance in-between your fingers.

✓ Relax your shoulders and take deep breaths.

✓ Start moving your hands very slowly, moving your palms closer and away from each other, without touching each other, ten to fifteen times.

✓ Gradually, you will feel as if you are moving your hands inside a bucket full of water. The current or flow which you will feel on your hands will vary at different places as the proportion of energy is different at different places.

✓ Now bring your palms again four inches closer to each other and very slowly start rotating them in clockwise motion, one after another, for ten to fifteen times. This will make you feel the male energy of the place.

✓ Now keeping the same position slowly start rotating your hands in anti-clockwise motion, one after another, for ten to fifteen times. This will make you feel the female energy of the place.

✓ You will observe that either the male or the female energy is dominant at different places depending upon the type of people present there or the type of worship happening there. If you are checking these energies on the top of the mountain, then you will find the female energy dominating the male energy. This may be the reason why Hindus created all their goddesses temples on mountain tops. The other reason is that women dominate among tribes living on the mountain tops around the world.

✓ Make a ball of the energy by pushing one palm, preferably the left one close to the other; you will feel a ball forming inside your right palm.

✓ Make the ball denser so that you can literally feel its weight in your hand or you can feel it bounce back in your palm, if you try and throw it up in the air.

✓ Take this ball of energy in both your palms, keeping your eyes open, place the palm on your eyes. This will help you gaze at a person or a thing placed in front of a white back ground without blinking your eyes. Do not stare, gaze. The best spot to gaze at is a person's third eye, in-between the eyebrows.

✓ Don't try to look around the person, look at the person, and within a few second you will see the Aura of that person.

✓ Now you can shift your attention to some other object or person placed in front of a white background and you will see the Aura of that person or thing.

✓ Please note that if you are trying to watch the Aura of a picture and the picture is of a dead person, you will not see any Aura around his or her picture, as dead people, and their picture, do not have an Aura.

✓ Be patient and confident, and you will start seeing the Aura.

✓ With more practice you will start seeing different colors, Chakra, sizes and shapes of Aura.

People who believe in simplicity, and have faith that they can see the Aura via this technique will surely start seeing the Aura, but those who have a concept that it is difficult to see the Aura with such an easy technique will have to go for the second option, which is difficult.

▶ **The Second technique of Gazing (Tratak) to see the Aura :**

✓ Get the chart you would find in the picture section of the book framed with a non-glaring glass.

✓ After doing your Pranayam and chanting Pranav for three times, sit comfortably and easily in a lightly lit, almost dark room having a white wall or background. Place the frame at a distance of seven to ten feet on the white wall so that the center spot is slightly higher than the eye level.

✓ Rotate your eyes very slowly around the picture in such a way that you can make an observation of every dimension from outward to inward in the chart.

✓ Looking at each and every line, circle, triangle or square in the chart, start from the top-outside end, slowly moving your eyeballs in clockwise movement going to the inner surface.

✓ When your attention reaches the center dot, keep your body relaxed and still, without blinking start gazing at the dot.

✓ In the first week, do this for five minutes.

✓ While you are gazing at the dot, slightly move your attention to the outer surface, concentrating at the center.

✓ You will see the Aura of the outer surface of the diagram.

✓ After a week, you can increase the time from five minutes to eight to ten minutes. Once you can do that, you can start practicing seeing the human Aura with help of technique one.

✓ This exercise will also increase your memory, concentration, will power and intuition.

✓ Please practice this only after doing Pranayam and Pranav chanting.

✓ Be sure that you don't rush to increase the time of Tratak, gradually increase five minutes per week.

✓ Do not go beyond thirty five minutes of gazing constantly.

✓ Do not practice gazing for more than twice a day.

✓ In warmer countries, reduce the gazing time as a lot of heat is aroused in the body by Tratak, and overheating of the system can cause health problems like acidity and anger.

Stop this practice, immediately if you find any kind of restlessness, difficulty, itching in eyes or if you feel giddy. If you still continue then the consequences sometimes might health threatening.

▶ Changes in the Aura

"Things are as they are,
it is you who label them as beautiful or ugly"

'Sri Sri Ravi Shankar'

Changes are seen in the Aura at different times and places for good or bad. These changes can be in terms of shape, size and colour of the Aura and Chakras.

▶ Negativity:

✓ Shapes forming in negativity: If you see a break in the oval shape of an Aura, then that negativity has started to enter that Aura. A perfect oval-shaped Aura means a pure Aura.

✓ Colours forming in negativity: If you see shades of black, grey, brown, sharp dirty green etc. then that the person is suffering from negativity and the body part where you see these patches is also affected with the same emotions.

✓ If you see black, charcoal, grey, muddy brown and pale pink together in a person's Aura, then that the person is suffering from a serious illness in that part of the body.

✓ Decrease in size of Aura in negativity: An average human aura has to be around four to five fingers i.e. approximately four to five inches big. A bigger Aura than five fingers, size indicates that the person is spiritually advanced, in good health, stress-free and negativity-free.

✓ A smaller Aura than the average size means the person is suffering from bad health, negativity and stress.

✓ If a pale Aura is lesser than three inches or finger's size then keep a constant watch on the person's Aura. If you see it decreasing, day by day, then it hints to a threat to the life of that person. In this kind of case do the following:

a. Ask the person to see a good doctor immediately.

b. Make him go through a proper session of Aura cleansing.

c. Ask the person or the person's relatives to chant the Maha-Mirtunjay Mantra (The ritual to win over death and diseases) or Maha-Mirtunjay Bij Mantra (The advance ritual to win over death and diseases) for thirty six thousand times. If it is not possible for them then either you do it for them after taking the Sankalp (determination) or get it done through someone knowledgable. The Maha-Mirtunjay Mantra, Maha-Mirtunjay Bij Mantra and the method of Sankalp is given below :

"None has the power to destroy the unchangeble"

'Swami Vivekanand'

◆ Maha-Mirtunjay Mantra:

"Aum Triambakam YajaMahe Sughandhim Pushti Vardhanam
Urva Rukmiva Bandhanat Mirtyor Mokshi Maa-amritat Aum

Meaning:

Aum O one with three eyes (one who can see all three tenses-past, present and future) I pray to thee, make me smell good and holistically healthy, like a bird or cucumber (immediately and effortlessly) free me from the bondages of death but not from the nectar of immortality Aum.

Maha-Mirtunjay Bij Mantra:

"Aum Houm Jhoum Saha Aum"

Chant the Maha-Mirtunjay Bij Mantra instead of Maha-Mirtunjay Mantra only if there is a difficulty in chanting Maha-Mirtunjay Mantra.

Starting on any good day, chant the above mantras for 36000 times in front of an energized and sanctified Maha-Mirtunjay Yantra. Males must complete it within 42 days and females in around 21 to 24 days, in-between their two monthly cycles.

• Blocks formed by negativity:

✓ The negativity causes blocks in the energy centers (Chakras) in the Aura.

✓ The negativity makes us dull, inattentive, dreamy, ill, depressed and inactive.

✓ These blocks can be seen by a clairvoyant or the person himself can feel them in form of illness, pain, phobia etc.

✓ They have to be attended to before they become old and deeply rooted in our system. It is easy to remove a new, big dark patch of negativity by Aura cleansing or Aura cleansing meditation, than removing an old small patch.

SECTION
4

1. VIBGYOR

"If we see the Rainbow we cannot see the Sun! It is same as if you can see God then the world will disappear and if you see the world you cannot see God!! But a person who has seen God can see the world better! and the person who has seen the Sun can see the Rainbow better! Here the Sun is your soul!!"

'Hittesh Morjaria'

✓ An expert who has practiced seeing the Aura for a long period one who is gifted to see the colours as a result of his or her's past life, practices, can see different colours in the Aura.

✓ A human Aura is like a living rainbow, every colour and shade of the Aura indicates nature, health, mood, surrounding, stress and much more.

✓ These different colours with their different shades allow an Aura reader to know what the person is thinking, where his energy is blocked, what kind of illness or stress will be there in the future, and what type of cleansing is required for the Aura.

✓ An Aura reader must be very careful while seeing the Aura. A person's Aura takes the colour of his or her clothes, makeup or also the surroundings. To judge the Aura colour perfectly, an expert must ask his subject to wear white clothes with white inner garments and sit in front of a white background without makeup. A good expert does not allow his notions to judge a person's Aura.

✓ Hinduism which accepts Godhood in all colours have Gods having white, golden, purple and even red or blue Aura colours (their meanings will be simplified in further chapters), which indicates anger, passion, mischief etc.

✓ There are many shades of one single colour, and every shade has its own meaning, which might be exactly opposite to another shade of the same colour.

✓ There are many false concepts about Aura and its colours. For instance, a person has the same colour Aura all his or her life, the size of the Aura hardly changes, one Aura colour is always dominant than others. Blue colour Aura means the person is highly spiritual, intelligent, trustworthy and honest; Green Aura means the person is very emotional and Red means anger or lust.

✓ A good Aura reader must be free of all types of concepts. Human Aura is such a vast subject that an Aura reader's whole life is not enough to be perfect in this subject. I learn something new every day with every case I read.

✓ A good Aura reader must never come to a random conclusion. Human Aura is like a human body, a very complex system; as it is ever changing in colour, shape and size as per our mental state.

✓ We can wear certain colours of clothes or makeup to change our Aura to that colour, so in return it can change our moods and thoughts. Like a short-tempered person must avoid orange and red shades and wear more whites and greens. A person who gets depressed or is easily affected by negativity must avoid wearing black and grey, whereas people looking for love and relationship must wear more pinks. You can also refer the colour chart (elsewhere in the book) to know which colour to wear. Wearing the colours to suit your moods was also recommended by famous Swiss psychiatrist Carl Jung.

✓ People wearing bright coloured clothes live longer than people wearing black and grey. This might be one of the reasons why women outlive men, and why men suffer more from heart diseases than women, though the other reason for this is because women cry a lot more than men thus never bottling up the feelings. It is the male ego which does not allow a man to cry. By crying a person relives a lot of suppressed emotions from the Aura which keeps the Aura clean.

✓ Black and grey colours also make a person tired very soon. It makes him look older before age.

✓ The theory of usage of colours is also called the colour therapy. The most important part of colour therapy is drinking water from different coloured glass or transparent bottles. This and other types of theories of colour therapy create a very strong impact on our Aura.These theories require a deep knowledge of shades of Aura, the person's life style and his astrological chart. Half knowledge of all this will lead to dangerous results.

2. Colours of Human Aura:

✓ Human Aura as we now know is the human mind. Our Mind or Aura is a product that connects energy to matter. It is the boundary line of energy and matter, and we can say it is the energy which creates matter.

✓ There are many properties of matter, one is the colour. Like a baby who has received everything he or she has from the parents, the matter too has is made of everything received its creator, the mind or Aura. So seeing the colours of the matter, is almost like seeing the Aura.

✓ Different colours of the Aura project different moods, feelings, past, present or future illness, negativity, depression etc.

✓ There are many misconceptions about human Aura colours, as they are generalized. The different shades of the Aura are more important than the colours for perfect interpretation. All good shades pleasing the eyes have a good effect and all dirty shades have negative effects. The colour of the Aura keeps on changing so they must not be understood as permanent. They only reflect a person's mood, thought and physical or mental order. It will be incorrect to label a person good or bad by his or her's Aura colour.

✓ These colours also show on human skin, so we connect different colours with different feelings like red with rage, yellow with fear, green with jealousy, purple with passion, blue with depression etc. However every colour with its variety of shades has profuse meanings associated with it.

✓ Beginners can associate red Aura with physical self for functions of the body like anger, sex, hard work etc., yellow Aura with mental self for functions of the mind like fear, knowledge, education etc.; and blue Aura with spiritual self for functions of the soul like meditation, bliss, depression etc.

✓ If an Aura reader is regular with his breathing (Pranayam) and meditation then he or she can start seeing different shades in the colours.

✓ It is not necessary that the colour or shade of the whole Aura will be the same throughout the body. You may also see patches of different colours and shades in it; especially the parts of black or grey negativity is very well seen in the Aura.

✓ There are nine basic colours out which Violet, Indigo, Blue and Green are cool colours; Yellow, Orange and Red are hot colours; White and black are neutral colours.

✓ This is the most basic and useful information for balancing Aura colours and shades via Aura cleansing.

✓ All the colours of VIBGYOR have come out of white colour, but when they are remixed you get black colour.

✓ Enlightenment or perfect Aura balancing is balancing all colours to give one perfect White.

✓ If the balancing is not done by an expert, it might cause more black negativity in the patient's Aura.

✓ When you can see the White Sun, you cannot see the VIBGYOR rainbow; and when you see the colourful VIBGYOR rainbow, you cannot see the White Sun.

✓ In the same manner, when a person is spiritually inclined, having a healthy mind, body and soul, he has sliver white rainbow of all seven colours as his or her's Aura colour. You will not see any other colours, but when you see different colours or shades, then the white is not seen.

3. The Meaning behind the Shades and the Colours of Aura:

"Knowledge of Death makes you immortal. It's wrong to say 'makes you immortal', it makes you aware that you are immortal anyway"

'Sri Sri Ravi Shankar'

► **White:**

We will start with the colour white and its shades; this colour is seen as transparent.

i.   A clear white is the Aura seen in a person after an Aura cleansing or a meditation process.

ii.   This colour indicates clear perception, good health, spirituality, faith, truthfulness and absence of negativity.

iii.   Wearing white brings you in total acceptance towards everyone and everything.

iv.   There is an adverse effect of wearing any colour, but there is no adverse effect of wearing white colour on the Aura, hence white colour clothes are accepted universally by all the religions.

v.   Now we will see the indication of different shades.

✓   **Hazy White:** It's seen when there is start of negativity or tiredness, or if the person is an orthodox.

✓   **Pale Light White:** It's seen in person close to death, it will be very difficult for this kind of person to recover.

✓   **Silver:** It's seen in a spiritually advanced person involved in regular practice or person having abundance or is also seen when a proper Aura cleansing is done on the person.

✓   **Cream:** It's seen when there is acceptance, tolerance, charm, grace and maturity in a person at that given time.

✓   **Ivory:** It's seen when the person has lost purity or wishes to move away from impure surroundings.

✓ **Off White:** It's a sign of active or restless mind slowly calming down.

✓ **Opal:** It's the Aura of a person starting something new with good faith in his or her heart.

✓ **Opaque:** Person is very focused at this moment.

✓ **Pearl:** Indicates person at peace.

✓ **Sea shell-:** It's an Aura of an inventor, scientist or a person doing research.

▶ **Red:**

Red colour indicates physical state; all gross emotions in life like anger, life-force, survival tendency, passion, sex, frustration, attraction, repulsion, non-forgiving, anxiety, nervousness, obsession, materialistic thoughts, resistance, high blood pressure or pulse rate, over physical strain, head strong, pride, change etc. are reflected in red colour.

i. Sometimes red Aura is also observed in women in their menstrual cycles and people suffering from common cold or fever.

ii. Some of the spiritual practitioners around the world wear red (not ochre or orange) to enhance their powers. These people wearing red, are either practicing in a field of occult which deals in sexual practices or a practice wanting to attract someone or worship of female deities, or a spiritual practice to exude your personality or sexuality.

iii. Wear red if you want to increase your sexual or physical energies, attract attention, warn people, do exercise or want a successful marriage. One of the ancient books of Astrology called the 'Lal Kitab' meaning 'The Red Book', suggests that a male must wear a red vest and female must wear a red bras.

iv. Avoid wearing red if you easily get aroused, or if you are not involved in much physical work.

v. In many countries people doing hard labor jobs, also wear red to boost their physical strength.

vi. A person who gets nervous easily or is short-tempered must avoid wearing red colour.

vii. Now we will see the indication of different shades.

✓ **Deep Red:** It's seen in people re-energizing, protecting themselves.

✓ **Cherry Red:** It's seen in people in love or relationship, especially if they are around their loved ones or a person who loves his or her own selve.

✓ **Bright Clear Red:** It's seen when there is high energy, but needs caution as it might turn into high blood pressure. Is also seen when the person is aware of his or her inner beauty, passion, will power, activeness, courage etc. But care needs to be taken as this colour might easily change to give high blood pressure or hyper activity.

✓ **Coral:** It's seen when a person is having new friends or healing from one-sided love.

✓ **Deep Magenta:** It's seen when a person is in compassion and caring.

✓ **Dirty Mud Red:** Says that the person is at present suffering from high blood pressure or hyper activity, or he is head strong, angry and aggressive.

✓ **Indian Traditional Red:** It shows leadership qualities in the owner.

✓ **Light Red:** It's seen when a person is over-whelmed and energized with courage or success.

✓ **Golden Red:** It's a colour of power received from Spiritual practices or rituals.

✓ **Brownish Red:** Indicates suppressed emotions or anger, which is seen generally around the head and needs immediate cleansing.

✓ **Very Dark almost Brown Red:** Tells you that the person has selfish desire or desires in his mind, to be careful of him or her.

✓ **Ruby Red:** Shows passion or anger around the face. Needs cleansing and breathing (Pranayam) exercise.

✓ **Claret (dark ruby) Red:** Tells you that the person is tensed and needs cleansing.

✓ **Ruddy or flushed or reddish yellow:** The person is passionate now but is shy to express.

✓ **Russet Red:** Says the owner is short-tempered always ready to fight and will change with regular meditation.

✓ **Tomato Red:** Indicates pride.

✓ **Violet Red:** Indicates passion, aroused by love.

✓ **Carmine Red:** Person is desperate for a change.

✓ **Vermillion:** Shows creativity in a person.

✓ **Scarlet (Burgundy) Red:** Owner is excited with passion or is hungry for people's attention.

✓ **Crimson (Cherry Pink) Red:** Person is stuck in grief or choices or anger mixed with sorrow needs cleansing of the heart (Anaahat), solar plexus and third eye (Aangya) chakra.

✓ **Deep Crimson:** Person is experiencing shame.

✓ **Maroon Red:** Says the owner is powerful yet self-centered.

✓ **Cloudy Red:** Person has cruel intentions, beware.

▶ **Violet :**

Many colours-Purple, Indigo, Wine, Lavender, Lilac, Magenta, Mauve, Burgundy and Grape fall in this category.

i. I have chosen Violet as their leader because it is the colour of the Sahastrar (Crown) Chakra.

ii. Violet Aura means the owner is a healer; he or she is at the pinnacle of spirituality, has strong intuitions and is a visionary, futuristic, idealistic, artistic and magical.

iii. It is also the colour of salvation or realization.

iv. Violet is also seen around a person after meditation. It also means that the owner is very sensitive towards others and this might cause some trouble for the owner.

v. If a person is using some spiritual aid or support systems like an energized and sanctified Crystal or a Rudraksh rosary then too the person's Aura turns Violet or Purple.

vi. Violet is more a mental colour opposite to red which is more of a physical colour.

vii. Violet mixed with Purple or Red is worn by many who are into healing professions like doctors or alternate therapists around the world.

viii. It helps in fast recovery by installing faith, calmness and bliss in the patients.

ix. Like other colours, even violet has its own negative effects like suppressed emotions, over-sensitiveness and day-dreaming, if it is seen in negative shades.

x. Make your patient wear violet if you want him to drop addictions or come out of a long misery, or pain.

xi. Do not suggest your patient to wear violet if he is a day dreamer and does not like physical jobs, as it will create more lethargy and dreaminess in him or her.

✓ **Purple:** A pure Purple Aura like the black negative Aura can rarely be seen all around the person. It is also seen for a very short time before it changes to some other colour.It indicates wisdom, intuitions, controlling people via psychic powers mixed with passion, a person having spirituality as passion.

✓ **Purple Violet:** Seen in devotees, especially in presence of a spiritual master (Guru).

✓ **Dark Purple:** Indicates a person is in deep meditative state or a person having strong intuition or vision. If there is a blackish effect in the dark Purple then it indicates the person has achieved deep meditative state or psychic powers with the help of intoxicants or drugs.

✓ **Light Purple:** The person is lucid dreaming.

✓ **Royal Bright Purple:** The person has developed spiritual energies to the fullest.

✓ **Light Violet:** The person has the power to charm others with ease and is in communication with the ethereal world.

✓ **Lavender:** says that the person has the knowledge of death, or the person is ready for his or her death without any fear.

✓ **Lilac:** It's a shade between blue and amethyst. It indicates balance in body and mind.

✓ **Magenta:** This is one colour used more in India; it indicates commercialized views in the owner, and the power to heal others.

✓ **Mauve:** Indicates that the owner is confident yet very humble. Again this kind of feeling arises mostly in the presence of the spiritual master.

✓ **Burgundy:** Indicates that the person is wealthy and elegant.

✓ **Indigo:** It's the colour of the third eye. It indicates the person is having powerful intuitions and multiple supernatural powers (Siddhi).

✓ **Dirty Indigo:** Indicates that the person is under a spell or is hypnotized and needs help immediately.

✓ **Grape:** Indicates that the person is too lazy right now.

✓ **Wine:** Indicates that the person has started responding to the therapies applied on him to cleanse his or her Aura.

► **YELLOW :**

Yellow is the colour of fear, nervousness and alertness. The positive effects of the Yellow Aura is that it reflects analytical thinking, pure child-like happiness and joy, sanguinity, detachment filled with life, not sorrow, sensitivity with detachment.

i. As it is the colour of the navel (Manipur) Chakra, it also indicates generosity and if seen with a negative shade especially of green, indicates greed or jealousy.

ii. Being the colour of Jupiter, it is also connected with spiritual development of a person.

iii. Yellow is the best colour to wear for prosperity, education and good luck, but if the person is too fearful, then he must avoid wearing Yellow colour.

✓ **Light Yellow:** States that the person is optimist or is agreeing to the situation. Or the person is shy.

✓ **Bright Lemon Yellow:** This means that the person is at the pinnacle of success or joy.

✓ **Lemon Yellow:** This means that the person is focused.

✓ **Dark Brownish Yellow :** Shows that the person is stressed and running out of time.

✓ **Dull Pale Yellow:** The person is experiencing fear.

✓ **Dark Yellow:** The person is starting to be disloyal, cruel, spineless, old, ill, doubting or jealous.

✓ **Primrose:** The person is jolly and in no doubt.

✓ **Pale Primrose :** The person is a thinker.

✓ **Buttercup Yellow :** The person is trying to be aware.

✓ **Golden Yellow:** The person is motivated.

✓ **Lemon :** It's seen during Aura cleansing process. It is a colour of cleansing taking place.

✓ **Mustard:** Indicates that the person is scheming against or is jealous of someone or something.

✓ **Sulphur:** The person is in physical or mental pain.

✓ **Sunlight Yellow:** The person is creative.

✓ **Straw Yellow:** The person is lost in his or her dream.

▶ **Golden Yellow:**

Some Aura readers believe that golden yellow does not have many shades, and some believe that all the colours that glitter are gold and will give the same effect, but that is not true.

i.   Golden yellow says that the person is free from all sorts of negativity and is on a very high level of consciousness.

ii. The person with the a Golden yellow Aura has minimum thoughts, strong faith and divine qualities.

iii. Golden yellow Aura also indicates prosperity and good health.

iv. Like the other Aura colours, some shades of Golden yellow Aura like Zinc and Copper indicate negativity.

v.   Wearing gold ornaments will be more useful than wearing golden yellow clothes but do not wear shades of gold if you are aroused easily, or you are practicing celibacy.

✓ **Royal Golden Yellow:** It's a sign that the person is leading a royal life.

✓ **Light Golden Yellow:** It's seen in a healthy and wealthy person.

✓ **Pure Golden Yellow:** It's an Aura of a spiritual giant.

✓ **Golden Orange:** Indicates that the owner was very short tempered earlier, but now with spiritual understanding and help, has transformed and channelized his anger.

✓ **Golden Topaz:** Indicates that the owner is contented with his or her achievements and success in life.

✓ **Golden Yellow:** Indicates that the owner is right now full of bliss.

✓ **Golden Brown:** It's an Aura of a wealthy person surrounded by mean friends.

✓ **Zinc:** Indicates that the person is provoked by sexual desires or anger.

✓ **Copper:** It's seen in labourers and coolies.

▶ **Orange:**

Orange is a colour of mental and physical strength. It is worn by Hindu and Buddhist saints, who travel the length and breadth of the earth on their foot and are involved in rigorous meditations and rituals.

i.   Orange is also a colour of rebelliousness, inspiration and bliss.

ii. This may be known to a few that Orange is also used to give shock treatments; a master creates a shock situation for his disciple, to enlighten and advance him. The Orange Aura of the disciple, which is highly supported by the orange and ocher clothes, gives him strength and acceptance to bear the shock.

iii. Orange is also a colour of festival. In India, it is the most used colour in decoration and cloth's for all the celebration. It indicates joy, warm-heartedness and awareness. It has been seen that the awareness is lost when a person is happy, but use of Orange allows both the opposites to exist together.

iv. Orange is the best colour to treat of mental illness, depression, fear, disgruntlement, cynicism, distrust and loss of appetite.

v. As it is the colour of the genital (Swadhisthan) chakra, many colour therapists and Aura readers believe that it is a colour which enhances physical desire and sensuality, but this is untrue. Swadhisthan Chakra though based at the genitals also helps in digestion. Mulaadhar Chakra is responsible for passion. On the contrary, Orange clothes help an aesthetic to rise above his physical desires, and maintain celibacy, to use the energy saved to move the Kundalini to the higher realms.

vi. Orange is also the colour of the earth. It blesses the individual with good health and vigor.

vii. Orange is also a colour of challenge, letting go and physical labor.

viii. Avoid wearing Orange, when you want to rest or when you are attending a funeral.

ix. Like other colours, even Orange has its own negative effects, if it is seen in negative shades.

✓ **Apricot:** Indicates that the person is admiring, respecting or in approval of someone.

✓ **Bright Orange:** indicates a strong flow of energy in the person.

✓ **Burnt Orange:** Says the person is an opportunist.

✓ **Pumpkin:** Indicates that the person is happy but also in control.

✓ **Amber:** Indicates that the person has attained supernatural powers.

✓ **Sienna:** Indicates that the person has control over his thoughts.

✓ **Cloudy Orange:** Indicates that the person is possessing supernatural powers without intellect and so might loose powers or misuse them in both the cases that might harm him or others around.

✓ **Dark Orange:** Indicates that the person is powerful, but still humble.

✓ **Light Orange:** Indicates that the person is powerful but shy.

✓ **Deep Orange:** Indicates that the person is a fanatic about his religious beliefs.

✓ **Muddy Orange:** Indicates that the person is on an ego trip.

✓ **Orange Brown:** Indicates that the person is having strength in the body but still is acting tired or lazy out of ignorance or hypocrisy.

✓ **Orange Red:** Indicates that the person is proud of his achievements, but he or she must be careful of passion or rage.

✓ **Orange Yellow:** Indicates that the person is moving his energies to higher realm.

▶ **Pink :**

Pink is the colour of love and happiness. The Pink Aura not only indicates that the person is unconditionally in love with the other, but also the person loves himself or the work or the surroundings that he is in.

i. If you want to spot the Pink Aura, you have to be around the youth. Teenage is an age when a person is in love with everything around. Pink Aura is difficult to be found among the middle-aged and working people who follow a routine.

ii. One common human value attached to Pink colour is the Smile. As kids and teenagers we smiled a lot, but as grown up, we forget to smile. If we are holding a post of great intelligence or honor, then it seems that it is a crime to smile.

iii. Pink Aura is also the colour of faith. If a pink Aura is observed, then it is sure that the person is faithful to the person he or she is with, but this loving Aura colour also has negative shades.

    iv.   Wearing pink colour increases affection, happiness, sensitivity, vulnerability. People start accepting and loving you more if you start wearing pink.

    v.   Avoid wearing pink if you are feeling vulnerable and insecure.

✓ **Pale pink:** Indicates that the person is beginning to fall in love.

✓ **Pink Madder:** Indicates that the person is faithful to his or her partner.

✓ **Salmon Pink:** Indicates that the person loves what he or she is doing.

✓ **Glistering Pink:** Indicates that the person is passionately in love.

✓ **Dirty Pink:** Indicates that the person will blindly trust anyone.

✓ **Dark Pink:** Indicates that the person is gentle and loving.

✓ **Deep Pink:** Indicates that the person is successful in love, generally seen in people about to marry or just married.

✓ **Fuchsia:** Indicates that the person is emotionally tensed.

✓ **Ivory Pink:** Indicates that the person is falling in love with a close friend of opposite sex.

✓ **Light Pink:** Indicates that there is love and romance in the air for the first time, the person feels like a virgin touched for the very first time.

✓ **Orchid Pink:** Indicates that the person is at the pink of health.

✓ **Peach:** Indicates that the person has the power to attract a crowd.

✓ **Pale Peach:** Indicates that the person is arrogant of his or her position.

✓ **Pink Red:** Indicates that the person is passionately in love.

✓ **Rose Pink:** Indicates that the person is in unconditional love with someone or himself.

▶ **Brown :**

Brown is considered a negative Aura colour, but all shades of brown are not negative. It is a colour of hard work and humility.

i. Brown is the colour of the soil, and so it is connected to hard work, modesty, commitment, determination, lack of money, loss of security, practicality, lack of goal.

ii. Brown colour Aura is generally seen in hard working and lower class people.

iii. Wear Brown when you need to really want to do some hard physical job, but do not wear Brown when you want to enjoy life.

✓ **Doe Skin:** Is seen when the person is very orderly. Sometimes the person can be much orderly for others to tolerate.

✓ **Mushroom:** Indicates that the person lives without dreams.

✓ **Fawn:** Indicates that the person is gradually coming out of his bad brown period.

✓ **Chocolate Brown:** Indicates that the person is in the field of agriculture or gardening.

✓ **Russet Brown:** It's an Aura colour of a laborer.

✓ **Dark Brown:** Indicates that the person's energy is drained and needs immediate Aura cleansing.

✓ **Grey Brown:** Indicates that the person thinks only of himself and no one else, not even his family.

✓ **Light Brown:** Indicates that the person is in a doubt.

✓ **Maroon:** It's an Aura of a person, who is in defence service. It is the colour of hard work, strength, bravery, discipline and sacrifice.

✓ **Russet Brown:** Indicates that the person is into a profession which requires hard physical labor.

✓ **Tan:** Indicates that the person is into a service field, or this Aura colour can also be a result of a sunbath.

✓ **Terracotta:** Indicates that the person is idiosyncratic.

✓ **All other earth colours like soil, wood etc.:** Indicates that the person is ego less, is either into a profession which requires hard physical labour or connected to farming or any of the field work which does not allow sitting in a closed room.

▶ **Black :**

Black Aura is generally brighter than the background and it glows. But if it is darker than the background, more like a smoke than a glow, then it indicates negativity. All these negative shades need cleansing.

i. Black is the most dangerous colour among all negative colours of Aura, and it needs proper reading and cleansing.

ii. It is the most easily noticed colour in the Aura, but a whole Aura surrounding a person's body or face is rarely seen completely black.

iii. If a complete Black Aura is seen in a person, then it is considered fatal and needs immediate cleansing.

iv. A complete Black Aura may be formed only due to the following reasons.

1. If an attempt has been made to kill the person with the help of black magic. This is the most common factor to form a total Black Aura.

2. If the person is unable to let go of some very old negative feeling like fear, hatred, anxiety, resentment, antipathy, antagonism, guilt, depression.

3. If a person is regularly abused in childhood.

4. If the person is going through a bitter event that he or she cannot handle, a like divorce or debt.

5.   If a person is a drug addict.

6.   If the person is practicing negative occult (Kal Tantra) with the Non-useable items (Makaar) or is in Devil or Satan worship.

v.   Except for the sixth point, all the above points require proper cleansing. I will not give any comment (good or bad) about the people with the spiritual belief of the sixth type, as everyone knows what is good or bad for them. I will only advice that you need a proper mentor to guide you through these practices and one mistake can be fatal for you and others around.

vi.   Black Aura like black colour does not allow any colour Aura to hold its identity with it, so there are no shades of Black Aura.

vii.   Avoid wearing black, unless you want to physically attract opposite sex, please Saturn or look thin. Always avoid wearing complete black and black undergarments unless needed for some kind of spiritual practices.

► **Grey :**

Grey is also one of the negative colours of the Aura. This is the only colour whose all shades have negative effects on a person.

i.   Grey colour Aura indicates negative thoughts, dullness, depression, unenthusiastic, subdued behavior, unfocused, stalemate, impasse, standoff, distrustful etc.

ii.   Avoid wearing grey unless you are suggested to wear them by an astrologer to correct your negative effects of planet Ketu.

✓   **Gloomy Grey:** Indicates the person has (a nasty mind) nastiness in his mind.

✓   **Light Grey:** Indicates that the person is right now experiencing fear. It requires immediate cleansing.

✓ **Yellow Grey:** Indicates the person will fall ill or the person is feeling fatiqued because of ill health. It requires immediate cleansing.

✓ **Blackish Grey:** Indicates that the person is going through depression. It requires immediate cleansing.

✓ **Dirty Grey:** Indicates that the person's Aura has amassed negative feelings like fears, desires, anger etc. which is now converting into phobias or health ailments. It requires immediate cleansing of the body and Chakra.

✓ **Dark and dirty Grey:** Indicates that the person has many energy blocks in the body-mind system. It requires immediate cleansing of the body and Chakra.

✓ **Blackish Grey, Brown and Light Pink together:** Indicates that the person will have fatal health ailments. It requires immediate cleansing of the body and Chakra.

▶ **Green:**

Green Aura is the colour of peace and tranquility. It calms a person from the core of the existence, the soul.

i.   The owner of this Aura has healing powers, is sensitive to other people's feelings, has intuitions, loves peace, has green fingers and is a quick thinker.

ii.   Like other colours, even some shades of green have negative effects like fears, jealousy, envy etc.

iii. Green is also an Aura colour of the Manipur Chakra, which indicates qualities like tenure and the will to posses. This leads to attributes like greed, jealousy and generosity.

iv.   Green Aura can cure you from ailments like eye diseases, stress, diabetes, ulcer, swelling, problems of the heart and lungs. It also helps in relaxing and detoxifying the body and reduces sexual attraction.

v.   You must wear Green clothes to heal or relax, reduce attention from opposite sex, to regenerate cells, to improve eye sight and memory. You must not wear green when you are in the field of art and fame as it brings out a lot of jealousy, if everything is sluggish and dormant in life.

vi.   People in art field can wear emerald (a green stone) only with diamonds around it or with an opal to compliment it.

✓   **Emerald Green:** Indicates that the person is grounded.

✓   **Bright Green:** Indicates that the person is having inspiring thoughts.

✓   **Dark dirty Green:** Indicates that the person is experiencing greed, jealousy, selfishness, lack of confidence, which might lead to illness. It requires immediate cleansing of the Aura, especially the stomach chakra.

✓   **Green Grey:**   Indicates that the person is experiencing fear as a result of envy or treachery, which might lead to illness. It requires immediate cleansing of the Aura and especially stomach chakra.

✓   **Jade:** Indicates that the person is very generous.

✓   **Pale Green:** Indicates that the person is sensitive, spiritual and compassionate; these people should be careful that their above mentioned points might turn around to be their weakness.

✓   **Lemon Green:** Indicates that the person is an impostor.

✓   **Lime Green:** Indicates that the person is only focused in earning though he may have enough.

✓   **Medium Green:** Indicates that the person is in the pink of health and has the ability to heal others.

✓ **Sea Green:** Is the best shade in Green Aura shades. It indicates that the person is a healer, sensitive towards others, is calm but at the same time dynamic, and always ready to help everyone.

✓ **Spring Green:** Indicates that the woman is expecting or wanting a child.

✓ **Mint Green:** Indicates that the person is happy with sudden or big profit.

✓ **Apple Green:** Indicates that the person is a healer.

✓ **Sparkling Green:** Indicates that the person is a party animal.

✓ **Jade:** Indicates that the person is kind and generous.

✓ **Viridian:** Indicates that the person is over sensitive, which might lead to illness. It requires immediate cleansing of the Aura, especially the stomach Chakra.

✓ **Olive Green:** Indicates that the person is a miser. It requires immediate cleansing of the body and stomach chakra.

✓ **Teal:** Indicates that the person is wise in decision and judgment.

✓ **Turquoise:** Indicates that the person has seen success slowly and gradually, before seeing success he has been through a very hard time. Such people value their success and everything they have received from it.

1. They have a capability of multi-tasking and organizing, but they get bored easily being in one field and doing the same thing for a long period.

2. They make good bosses and leaders.

3. Turquoise is a mixer of blue and green, the colour of throat and heart Chakra. People with Turquoise Aura have the capability to speak from their heart to make people relate and obey them.

4. People with Turquoise Aura are always willing to go out of their way to help others.

5. Wear Turquoise clothes to make your immune system strong, good communication skills, success in media field, to be of use to others and to help your eyes.

6. Wear the semi-precious stone Turquoise in your wrist to save you from arms and ammunitions, to save you from allergies, to enhance your immune system, to overcome fear and to have a sparkle in your eyes.

7. Wear the semi-precious stone in your neck closer the throat, if you are into a profession, which requires a lot of talking or voice modulation, media or art and service industry.

8. Do not wear Turquoise clothes or stone if you are over stretching yourself to help others. Mind you, you need to give attention to your self too.

9. Do not wear Turquoise stone if you have a hard hair growth and are facing problems in shaving yourself. It does not allow any weapon to work easily on you and makes your hair even harder.

✓ **Dark Turquoise :** Indicates that the person loves his own company and likes to live and work alone. Generally, these kind of people are artistic and very sensitivity.

✓ **Green Yellow :** Indicates that the person is going through jealousy, anger, conflict or fear which will lead him to illness. It requires immediate cleansing of the Aura, especially the stomach chakra.

▶ **Blue :**

Blue Aura colour represents devotion, masculine energy, guilt, gratitude and depression.

i.   Blue is the colour of the throat (Vishuddhi) Chakra.

ii. People having Blue Aura are deep thinkers.

iii. Blue Aura colour is also a soothing and peace colour. It is difficult for this kind of person to be angry.

iv. Blue Aura is also the colour of space, so it says that the person is spaced-out or in deep meditation.

v. As per the Hindu faith, it is the Aura colour of enlightened souls like Shiva and Krishna, that represents pure knowledge.

vi. Blue Aura minimizes pain, helps the nervous system and tranquilizes a person to heal him or her.

vii. Like Turquoise, Blue Aura helps in communica-tional skills, and evolves the the thought process.

viii. Negative shade of Blue Aura can cause problems in the legs.

ix. Wear Blue colour clothes to be organized, relaxed, isolated, tranquilized, recover from headaches, migraines, pains, cramps, stomach problems and vertigo.

x. Do not wear Blue colour when you are feeling depressed or lonely.

xi. Do not wear Blue Sapphire without consulting an expert astrologer as it has been seen, that the wearer might either lose everything he possesess or might lose a limb.

xii. Do not wear semi-precious stone Amethyst if you are lazy, and do not want to sleep more.

✓ **Soft Blue:** Indicates that the person is at peace or in meditative state.

✓ **Light Blue:** Indicates that the person is having faith and virtue which leads him to inner peace.

✓ **Electric Blue:** Indicates that the person is right now using supernatural power of telepathy or reading someone's mind.

✓ **Blue Grey:** Indicates that the person is having fear of the future. It requires immediate cleansing of the Aura, especially the throat Chakra.

✓ **Midnight Blue:** Indicates that the person is having divine protection after he or she has lost the battle and respect.

✓ **Navy Blue:** Indicates that the person is having self-pity and guilt and requires immediate cleansing of the Aura and especially throat Chakra.

✓ **Pale Blue:** Indicates that the person is over-sensitive and requires immediate cleansing of the Aura, especially the throat Chakra.

✓ **Pilot Blue:** Indicates that the person is protected from many types of negativity and black magic.

✓ **Prussian Blue:** Indicates that the person is in harmony with the surrounding.

✓ **Blue Purple:** Indicates that the person is inspirational and optimistic.

✓ **Blue Violet:** Indicates that the person is at the pinnacle of spirituality.

✓ **Azure Blue:** Indicates that the person is speaking or acting out of intuitions.

✓ **Bright Royal Blue:** Indicates that the person is a clairvoyant.

✓ **Dark Blue:** Indicates that the person is a 'Blue star'. This means the person lives in illusion and fantasizes things. He or she cannot channelize his energies and is wasting them in the wrong direction. This type of situation generally arises when a person has gone through a long mental trauma or doing wrong types of meditation without proper guidance from a Guru. This requires immediate attention of an expert and proper balancing of all Chakra; if the person is not meditating, he/she must be guided through proper and regular meditating process. The compact disc given with this book. But if the person is meditating, he/she must be made to stop all meditation and meet an expert Guru.

✓ **Muddy Blue:** Indicates that the person is in non-acceptance of the reality. This requires immediate cleansing of the Aura and especially the throat Chakra.

✓ **Delft Blue:** Indicates that the person is having strong principles, which might cause problems to him or others.

✓ **Amethyst:** Indicates that the person is not interested in material world and is ready to renounce.

✓ **Aqua:** Indicates that the person is a naturopath.

✓ **Sky Blue:** Indicates that the person is a psychic.

✓ **Ultramarine:** Indicates that the person lives or works near or on the sea, generally seen in sailors and people at a beach holiday.

✓ **Silver Blue:** Indicates great wisdom in the owner.

✓ **Steel Blue:** Indicates that the person is feeling cheated.

✓ **Sapphire Blue:** Indicates that the person is in depression.

▶ **VIBGYOR (rainbow colour) :**

I first knew about the VIBGYOR Aura in one of my training sessions. One of my students could see a rainbow in my Aura, which was followed by everyone claiming to see a rainbow.

i.   After the session, I tried to see my Aura in the mirror and around my limbs. I could see no Rainbow; I was a little worried as every student of mine could not have been wrong.

ii.   Determined to find the truth, after a long research, I did the same meditation before my students to see my rainbow Aura and was amazed that the VIBGYOR Aura showed up.

iii. I tried to make my students go through the same meditation and see the result, but only a few who were regular with their meditation practice could achieve the VIBGYOR Aura.

iv. With regular research, I came to the following conclusion VIBGYOR Aura and its owners as given below:

✓ VIBGYOR Aura is like seven stripes of rainbow seen after four to five inches of white Aura around the head and the limbs.

✓ VIBGYOR colour Aura is not permanent Aura. It appears only after meditation, which is followed by physical exercise, and a strict routine of proper diet and living.

✓ VIBGYOR Aura appears in a person who has practiced Asthang Yoga, i.e. eight limbs of yoga, which includes some do's and don'ts, physical exercise, breathing exercise, concentration, deep concentration, losing one's identity and meditation--- correctly.

✓ VIBGYOR Aura appears in a person who has supernatural powers (Siddhi), and uses them to help people.

✓ VIBGYOR Aura can be lost if the person loses connection with the thy self.

✓ Person having the VIBGYOR Aura has all his chakras active and has a chance to be enlightened in this life, or is already enlightened.

4. Effect on Aura Colours:

Astrology & Colours

As per Astrology, there are nine main planets and these nine planets have their Aura of different colours and they dominate different days. Thus it is advisable to wear different coloured clothes on different days or wear different coloured clothes to enhance the positive effects of the planets. Here's how.

▶ **Sun**

Sun is the king of all the planets. It is in the center of the solar system.

✓ Sun is the presiding planet for the constellation sign Leo.

- ✓ It stays in each constellation for a month. It is the main source for (Prana) the Aura or the vital breath energy, which keeps everything alive on the planet and the rains, which is the source of fresh water on earth.
- ✓ It affects food, metal, especially gold, politics, fame, petroleum etc.
- ✓ Sun makes a person famous, egoistic, powerful and angry.
- ✓ Sun presides the day Sunday. Sun presides over colours red, yellow, golden and orange.
- ✓ All red coloured stones specially the ruby are the stones to enhance the power of sun.

► **Moon**

Moon is considered to be the queen of all the planets.

✓ It is nearest to the earth.

✓ Moon is the presiding planet for the constellation sign Cancer.

✓ It stays in each constellation for two and a quarter days.

✓ It is the source of mind and creativity. It affects seeds, medicine, travel, water, thoughts, sleep and emotions.

✓ Moon makes a person artistic, original, beautiful, lazy, travel-prone and an insomniac.

✓ Moon presides the day Monday. Moon presides over colours white, silver, off-whites and light green.

✓ All white-coloured stones especially pearl and the moonstone are the stones to enhance the power of moon.

► **Mars**

Mars is considered to be the warrior among the planets.

✓ It is red in colour, is the presiding planet for the constellation signs Aries and Scorpio.

✓ It stays in each constellation for one and a half months.

✓ It is the source of energy and power.

✓ It affects seeds, property, machineries, electricity, vehicles and warriors or people working with armed forces.

✓ Mars presides the day Tuesday. Mars presides over colours orange and red colours.

✓ Many orange and red-coloured stones specially the red or orange coral and carnelian are the stones to enhance the power of Mars.

▶ **Mercury**

Mercury is considered to be the son of Moon.

✓ It is green in colour.

✓ It is the presiding planet for the constellation signs Gemini and Virgo.

✓ It stays in each constellation for One month.

✓ It is the source of energy and power.

✓ It affects all five senses plus memory, writers, bankers and businessmen.

✓ Mercury presides the day Wednesday. Mercury presides over colour green.

✓ Many green-coloured stones especially jade and emerald are the stones to enhance the power of Mercury.

▶ **Jupiter**

Jupiter is considered the mentor of all the deities and seers.

✓ Jupiter is also considered to be the knowledge of Kaal-Purush.

✓ In the solar system it is considered to be the minister.

✓ It is considered to be a very auspicious planet.

✓ It is the presiding planet for the constellation signs Sagittarius and Pisces.

✓   It stays in each constellation for one year.

✓   It affects yellow pulses, gold, turmeric, books, education, horses and spirituality.

✓   Jupiter presides the day Thursday. Jupiter presides over colour yellow.

✓   All yellow-coloured stones, especially yellow sapphire, golden topaz and citrine are the stones to enhance the power of Jupiter.

▶ Venus

Venus is considered an auspicious planet.

✓   It controls love, passion, art and creativity in our life; it blesses us with a life partner, kids and luxuries such as vehicles.

✓   Venus is the mentor of the demons and protects them via his Maha Mirtyunjay Sanjivani art.

✓   Venus is also known to be the greatest expounder of all the scriptures.

✓   It is the presiding planet for the constellation signs Taurus and Libra.

✓   It stays in each constellation for one month.

✓   It affects silver, gold, white horses, butter, camphor, curd, sugar, cows, potatoes, diamonds, expensive clothes, art, beauty, relationship, sex, perfumes etc.

✓   Venus presides the day friday. Venus presides over colours pink, purple and off-white.

✓   All off-white and transparent stones, especially diamond and opal are the stones to enhance the power of Venus.

▶ Saturn

Saturn is the most feared and misunderstood planet.

✓   He is the son of Sun and Chayaa (shadow). He is the elder foster brother of Yama (the deity of death) and Yamuna (the holy river).

✓ It is considered to be the account keeper of our karmas.

✓ It controls both health and wealth.

✓ It is the presiding planet for the constellation signs Capricorn and Aquarius.

✓ It stays in each constellation for two and half years.

✓ It affects leather, sesamine oil, iron, footwear, black pulses, buffalo, black cow, black and blue clothes, blue sapphire and all blue stones.

✓ Saturn presides the day Saturday. Saturn presides over blue and black colours .

✓ All blue and black stones especially blue sapphire, and opal are the stones to enhance the power of Saturn.

▶ **Rahu**

Rahu is also one of the most feared and misunderstood planets.

✓ He is the Chayaa Graha (shadow planet).

✓ He is known as the north lunar node.

✓ He is considered to have the body of a serpent and a terrifying face.

✓ He is the son of Simhikaa who is the wife of Viprachitiki and daughter of Hiranyakashyap.

✓ Hiranyakashyap was a mythological demon king killed by one of the incarnations of Vishnu.

✓ By his mother's name Rahu is also known as Simhike.

✓ He stays in each constellation for one and half years.

✓ He affects wool, bronze, photography, black clothes, black stones, black pulses, oil, black horse, accidents, thefts, court cases, physical problems etc.

✓ Rahu presides none of the weekdays but Wednesday and Saturday are good days to counter negative effects of Rahu.

✓ Rahu presides over colours brown and black.

✓ All brown and black stones, especially garnet, tiger eye, tiger iron, black tourmaline, aqua black agate and onyx are the stones to enhance the power of rahu.

▶ **Ketu**

Ketu is also one of the most feared and misunderstood planets.

✓ After Rahu's head was cut by Vishnu's Sudharshan Chakra, his body was known as Ketu.

✓ He is known as the south lunar node.

✓ The comets are also known as Ketu.

✓ As per Matsya Puran, there are many forms of Ketu. Dhum Ketu is the most important.

✓ Like Rahu, Ketu too is a Chayaa Graha (shadow planet).

✓ Ketu is considered milder than Rahu, but Ketu is also known as one of the Rudras, the fiercest incarnation of Lord Shiva.

✓ He looks like a flag in the sky, so its sign is a flag.

✓ He stays in one constellation for one and a half years.

✓ He affects poverty, looks, skin, genital and nail problems, kids, dogs, liberation etc.

✓ Ketu presides none of the weekdays but Tuesday and Sunday are good days to counter negative effects of Ketu.

✓ Ketu presides over colour grey.

✓ Cats eye is the stone to enhance the power of Ketu.

The chart below will help you with what colour clothes to wear on which day and which is the presiding planet.

Day of the week	Colours to be worn	Presiding planet
Sunday	Red, Yellow, Golden and Orange	Sun
Monday	White, Silver, Off-Whites and Light Green	Moon
Tuesday	Orange, Red or combination of Black & White	Mars Ketu
Wednesday	Green, Brown	Mercury Rahu
Thursday	Yellow	Jupiter
Friday	Pink, Purple and Off-White	Venus
Saturday	Blue	Saturn

Making it a practice to wear specific coloured clothes on the different days of the week as mentioned in the chart above, enhances your Aura. It allows the Aura to absorb positive energy from the planets and surroundings, which in return will grant you success and happiness.

► **Numerology and Colours**

There are ten single numbers in our counting system that also affect our Aura.

✓ **'Zero'** is an infinite number, and so it has no presiding planet or colour. Rest of all the numbers are connected with different planets and so it is also important that we take care of wearing the clothes, colours as per the dates of the month alongwith the weekdays. For this, we will need to see the characteristics of all the nine numbers.

✓ **One** is the first number. Its presiding planet is the Sun. (Please see the characteristics of the Sun for more details.) Each one born on any date with the total of 'One' i.e. the 1st, 10th, 19th or 28th of any month are influenced by the Sun as well as number 'One'. These people and others too, must prefer wearing Red, Yellow, Golden and Orange on Sundays and all dates adding to a total of 'One'.

✓ **Two** is the second number. Its presiding planet is the Moon. (Please see the characteristics of the Moon for more details). People born on any date with the total of 'Two' i.e. the 2nd, 11th, 20th or 29th of any month are influenced by the Moon as well as number 'Two'. These people should prefer wearing White, Silver, Off-Whites and Light Green on Mondays and all dates adding to a total of 'Two'.

✓ **Three** is the third number. Its presiding planet is Jupiter. Please see the characteristics of the Jupiter for more details. People born on any date with the total of 'Three' i.e. the 3rd, 12th, 21st or 30th of any month are influenced by the Jupiter as well as number 'Three'. These people should wear Yellow on Thursdays and all dates adding to a total of 'Three'.

✓ **Four** is the fourth number. Its presiding planet is Rahu. Please see the characteristics of the Rahu for more details. People born on any date with the total of 'Four' i.e. the 4th, 13th, 22nd or 31st of any month are influenced by the Rahu as well as number 'Four'. These people should prefer wearing Green or brown on Wednesdays and all dates adding to a total of 'Four'.

✓ **Five** is the fifth number. Its presiding planet is Mercury. (Please see the characteristics of the Mercury for more details). People born on any date with the totals of 'Five' i.e. the 5th, 14th or 23rd of any month are influenced by the Mercury as well as number 'Five'. These people should wearing Green on Wednesdays and all dates adding to a total of 'Five'.

✓ **Six** is the sixth number. Its presiding planet is Venus. (Please see the characteristics of the Venus for more details). People born on any date with the total of 'Six' i.e. the 6th, 15th or 24th of any month are influenced by the Venus as well as number 'Six'. These people should prefer wearing Pink, Purple and Off-White on Fridays and all dates adding to a total of 'Six'.

✓ **Seven** is the seventh number. Its presiding planet is Ketu. (Please see the characteristics of the Ketu for more details). People born on any date with the total of 'Seven' i.e. the 7th, 16th or 25th of any month are influenced by the Ketu as well as number 'Seven'. These people should wear combination of Black and White on Tuesdays and all dates adding to a total of 'Seven'.

✓ **Eight** is the eighth number. Its presiding planet is Saturn. (Please see the characteristics of the Saturn for more details). People born on any date with the total of 'Eight' i.e. the 8th, 17th or 26th of any month are influenced by the Saturn as well as number 'Eight'. These people should wear Blue on Saturdays and all dates adding to a total of 'Eight'.

✓ **Nine** is the ninth number. Its presiding planet is Mars. (Please see the characteristics of the Mars for more details). People born on any date with the total of 'Nine' i.e. the 9th, 18th or 27th of any month are influenced by the Mars as well as number 'Nine'. These people should wear Orange, and Red on Tuesdays and all dates adding to a total of 'Nine'.

The chart in the next page will give a reference of what coloured clothes should be worn on days of the week falling on particular total of dates of the month to enhance the Aura.

Dates	Sunday	Monday	Tuesday	Wednesday	Thursday	Friday	Saturday
1 10 19 28	Red Yellow Golden Orange	Yellow White Off- Whites	Red Orange	Light -Brown Green	Yellow	Pink Purple Red	Light- Blue
2 11 20 29	Yellow White	White Silver Off- Whites Light- Green	Yellow White Orange	White Off- Whites Light- Green	Yellow White	Pink White Off- White	White Light- Blue
3 12 21 30	Yellow White Golden	Yellow White	Yellow Orange	White Green	Yellow	Yellow Off- White Purple	Light- Blue
4 13 22 31	Red Brown	Light- Brown White	Red Brown	Brown Green	Yellow Brown	Off- White Light- Brown	Blue Purple Brown Black
5 14 23	Yellow	Light- Green White	Orange	Green	Yellow Green	Off- White Purple	Blue Light- Brown
6 15 24	Red Orange	White Off- Whites	Orange Red Pink Purple	White Green	Yellow	Pink Purple Off- White	Blue Purple
7 16 25	Yellow Golden	Off- Whites Whites	Black & Whites Purple	White Green	Yellow	Pink Purple Off- White	Blue Black
8 17 26	Yellow White	Off- Whites White	Purple Orange Red	White Green	Yellow White	Pink Purple White	Blue
9 18 27	Orange Red	Off- Whites White	Orange Red	White Green	Yellow Orange	Pink Purple	Blue Purple

✓ Please note that a person must not wear all black on any of the days . And if one should, black must be combined with any other colour.

✓ People whoare affected by depression, negativity and illness very easily and fast must avoid Black, Grey and Dirty Brown.

✓ People who experience fear very easily must avoid Pale Yellow.

✓ People with bad temper must avoid Red and Orange.

▶ **Name and Aura Colour :**

Like the planets, the days of the week and numbers even your name dominates your Aura.

✓ Every alphabet is connected to a number and as we have seen before, every number has its own colour.

✓ It is very important on how you spell your name, as this will tell you which Aura colour is dominant in you.

✓ Every time your name is called, the vibrations and colours dominant in your name show up in your Aura. It also decides your destiny and karma.

✓ The chart below presents the values of the alphabets and their colours.

No.	ALPHABETS	COLOUR
1	A – I – J – Q – Y	Golden Red
2	B – K – R	White
3	C – G – L – S	Yellow
4	D – M – T	Brown
5	E – H – N – X	Green
6	U – V – W	Pink
7	O – X – Z	Grey
8	F – P	Blue
9	--------------	Orange

Here's how we calculate and judge domination of Aura colour by the name of the person. For example:

>   Name: Hittesh Morjaria
>   DOB: 02 – 01 – 1972
>   Lucky no.   2
>   Destiny no. 4
>   Lucky colour as per lucky number White and Light Green.

Alphabet	H	I	T	T	E	S	H
Number	5	1	4	4	5	3	5
Colour	Green	Golden	Brown	Brown	Green	Yellow	Green
M	O	R	J	A	R	I	A
4	7	2	1	1	2	1	1
Brown	Grey	White	Golden	Golden	White	Golden	Golden

Result:

✓   Numerical total of the name is 1, so the colour of the full name is Golden; it means the person is connected to the Sun and has qualities of the Sun. Golden colour will be dominant in the Aura.

✓   The name has three Green alphabets, five Golden alphabets, two Brown alphabets, One Yellow alphabet and one Grey alphabet. It means that Golden colour will be dominating again, and the person has to be careful about the Brown and the Grey.

✓   Total of the birth date is 2, so the colour of his lucky date is White and Light Green; it means the person is also connected to the Moon and has qualities of the Moon. White and Light Green colours will be dominant in the Aura.

Summary :

My name and date of birth has domination of colour Golden, White and Light Green, so every time when my name is called, written or signed in my presence then I will feel the effects of this three colours, and their effects will be as follows: Golden, which is the most dominant, will keep me spiritually inclined, free from negativity, and famous. White will keep me pure and in 100% acceptance. Light Green will maintain sensitivity and also make me a good writer. White and Green together will not allow ego from the Golden colour to take over. Yellow brings the desire to help others, but I have to guard myself from sudden accidents I may face, because of the Brown and, over-sensitivity which might lead to depression.

Now let us calculate domination of Aura colour by the name of Isha, she is my student and very successful as an Aura reader and Astrologer:

Name: Isha (She does not use her full name)
DOB: 26 – 02 – 1985
Lucky no.   8
Destiny no. 6

Lucky colour as per lucky number Blue and shades of Blue but as 8 is a number which brings a lot of hurdles she also has to consider 6 with 8, so a mixer of Blue and Pink i.e. Violet and Purple will be lucky for her.

Alphabet	I	S	H	A
Number	1	3	5	1
Colour	Golden	Yellow	Green	Golden

Result:

✓   Numeric total of name is 1 so the colour of the full name is Golden; it means the person is connected to the Sun and has qualities of the Sun. Golden colour will be dominant in the Aura.

✓   The name has three Golden alphabets, one Green alphabet and One Yellow alphabet. It means that Golden will be dominating again, and the person will be helped by green and yellow to maintain her calm, to help people and to grow in spirituality.

✓   Total of the birth date is 8 but the colour of her luck number is Blue is not seen in the name so the person will be free of obstacles whenever her name is called, Pink colour of her destiny number 6 also does not appear in the name so the person will not allow relationship hinder her spiritual growth.

Summary

Isha's name has domination of colour Golden, Yellow and Green, so every time when her name is called, written or signed in her presence then she will feel the effects of this three colours, and their effects will be as follows: Golden, which is the most dominant, will keep her spiritually inclined, free from negativity, and famous. Green will maintain sensitivity and will not allow ego from the golden to take over. Yellow brings the desire to help others, but she has to guard herself from fear and jealousy triggered by Yellow and Green.

SECTION
5

1. Aura Cleansing

"My purpose is to deprogramme you, to clean you,
to uncondition you and leave you fresh, young and innocent.
And from there you can grow into a real authentic individual"

'Osho'

✓ We are all born with a clean Aura, which is innocent, loving, caring, faithful, spiritual and honest. But by the time, we come in contact with the outside world where there are different frequencies of different types of Auras, our Aura begins to lose its positive colours. No matter however positive the colour of other person's Aura may be, if it does not gel with our Aura, it makes our Aura impure.

✓ Impure means two thing which are together but are not of same type. For example, mix sugar with milk, sugar dissolves and keeps the milk pure; but if you mix oil with milk you will get impure oil as well as impure milk as none will dissolve.

✓ Impurity by non-acceptance creates conflicts, which in turn gives rise to more negativity caused by attachment, entanglement, desire, lust, greed, jealousy, anger, arrogance etc.

✓ Like our body, our Aura requires cleansing. There are some easy techniques to cleanse the impurities from your Aura on regular basis, but if you have a serious problem then you need a proper Aura cleansing session. If the Aura is badly affected with impurities then the Aura cleansing session will take a longer time and more than one session. It is suggested that you take someone's help to do the Aura cleansing to remove impurities.

▶ **For regular cleansing of Aura** from the impurities can be done as explained below :

✓ Following the disciplines mentioned in Chapter 7.

✓ Bathing with Aura cleansing salts daily.

✓ Using Aura cleansing herbal face pack.

✓ Practicing, breathing exercise and Yoga.

✓ Regularly practice Aura cleansing meditation.

✓ Wearing clean clothes.

✓ Using mood-enhacing perfume.

✓ Burning incense sticks or burning oil of lemon, sambarani, loban, eucalypts and Evils Eyes. This will not only cleanse your Aura but also the Aura of the room and everyone present in the room.

✓ Fill quarter of the bucket hot water, add a spoon of Aura cleansing salt of Evils Eye flavor and two fistful of rock salt to the hot water, sit with your feet dipped in it for half an hour. During this period, make sure that you feel happy, can read, watch television or work on your computer, but make sure you only do things which will make you feel happy and not excited, feverish, scared or sad.

▶ **Aura Cleansing Process:** To do this, it's necessary to free your mind from negativity energies like, anger, black magic etc. It is important for an individual to be free from the past and to attract positive people and situation in life.

You must not volunteer to cleanse anyone's Aura if:

✓ You are not meditating regularly.

✓ Your system is very sensitive and you get affected by negativity very easily and quick.

✓ You are suffering from negativity.

✓ You are unwell.

▶ **Important rules to be followed by the Aura cleanser during Aura cleansing:**

✓ Do not touch the patient if he or she does not like to be touched. This may take more than one an a half hours, so let

Archive

I would like to quote one of my celebrity clients, Dilip Mehra here.

"My daughter Radhika used to have cold, cough and fever every now and then. Once while visiting Mukteshwar Temple at Juhu Mumbai with my family, Hittesh Morjaria, a personal friend, saw my daughter and made an important observation that Radhika's Aura can be improved, which will further enhance her good health. Since I was worried about her weak health I asked him the remedy. To my surprise, he suggested a very simple and inexpensive procedure, which was to bathe her with crystal sea salt water adding Hittesh Morjaria's own branded Aura cleansing salt to it. He also suggested her to wear Evil's Eye stone.

I followed both of his suggestions and to day Radhika is doing fine. Thanks to Sri Sri Radha Krishna and my dear friend Hittesh Morjaria.

After this miracle, from being just an acquaintance, he became my friend, philosopher and guide.

In the weeks that followed, I had started to follow his guidance (which is based on scientific calculations and faith in God) similar Aura remedies for many of my big, small problems and decisions of daily life. He is always there in my hour of need, which is such a big relief because, in this hectic life we all want a pillar of help and support.

the patient be comfortable, let him or her lie down or sit on an easy chair. Aura does not open up to release negativity if the patient is not comfortable with you.

✓ You and your patient must breathe correctly throughout the Aura cleansing process. Ensure when you breathe in the stomach comes out and when you breathe out the stomach goes in. Eighty percent of toxins and waste of our body comes out through the breathe and twenty percent through stool, urine, eyes, nose, ears and mouth. Breathing is the best cleanser of Aura; wrong breathing pattern takes in negativity in your Aura while the correct way releases negativity.

✓ You and your patient must not wear anything black during the Aura cleansing process. The colour black absorbs negativity and does not allow it to flow out of the Aura.

✓ Make sure that your patient does not cross his hands, legs or fingers during the cleansing process, as that will stop the negative energy from flowing out.

✓ Ask the patient to wear loose cotton clothing, avoid tight clothes like under garments and silk, satin, wool or leather. Our body needs to breathe. The above mentioned clothes will not allow it to do so, thus creating an obstacle for Aura cleansing.

✓ Ask the patient to maintain distance in-between the hands and the legs, and let the palms face the ceiling in Chin Mudra. This will help in proper breathing.

✓ Make sure that you are in direct contact with the floor that you are standing on; this will absorb negativity that you absorb from the patient and give your positive energy.

✓ If you feel uncomfortable, sick or restless during the Aura cleansing process, stop the process immediately and take an expert's advice.

✓ You and your patient must take a bath with water mixed with Aroma Aura cleansing salts, immediately after the process.

✓ You and your patient must not eat or drink anything during and immediately after Aura cleansing process. Eat or drink only after taking bath.

✓ You and your patient must not apply oil, cream or any kind of sticky substance on your body or hair during the Aura cleansing process.

✓ The material used for Aura cleansing process must immediately be disposed.

✓ No other person except you and your patient must be present in the room where you are conducting the session. If there are people around, they will absorb negativity coming from the patient.

✓ Do not allow kids to enter the room in which you have done Aura cleansing till the next day. They have a soft and sensitive Aura which absorbs negativity really fast.

✓ Do not allow the mind to wander during the Aura cleansing session; cleansing happens when you are 100% focused.

✓ Keep cracking jokes and keep the atmosphere light. If you detect a serious illness in the patient then do not alarm him. Slowly suggest to him to see a doctor, Aura leansing is effective only when the patient is 100% relaxed.

✓ It is always advisable for you and the patient to perform an Aura cleansing meditation before and after the the process.

✓ Aura cleansing process cannot be done in a hurry, you need to give more time to the affected parts and Chakras. If needed, you must arrange for more than one session the next day.

✓ Always cleanse the Chakra from bottom to top. Start with the base Chakra and end with the Crown.

✓ Always remember to close the Aura at the end of the session.

▶ **Material:**

> *"There must be something strangely sacred in Salt.*
> *It is in our tears and in the Sea"*

'Khalil Gibran'

Use of appropriate material with mantra is necessary for an effective Aura cleansing.

✓ It is always better to start Aura cleansing with flowers and end it with a fire and peacock feathers.

✓ Except for the semiprecious stone pencils, no other material for Aura cleansing must be reused.

✓ Stone pencils must be cleansed properly before and after use.

✓ Material must be disposed off outside the house, and must not be kept in the garbage bag.

✓ Use appropriate material to balance the Tatwa. For example, never use red chilies or fire material for people who are short-tempered.

Material	Useful for purpose	Mantra to be chanted during the cleansing	Special note
White flowers	Opening the Aura, removing mental stress	Shiva or alternatives from any religion	Necessary to start with flowers for all types of problems
Red flowers	Opening the Aura, removing negativity	Siddha Kunjika	For all chakras below the solar
Blue flowers	Opening the Aura, removing obstacles & black magic	Shani	Good for Saturn period
Yellow flowers	Remove legal problems, stagnancy & paralytic attack	Baglamukhi Seed	Do not wear black
Orange flowers	Remove depression	Vishnu Seed	With total joy
Green Leaves	Remove depression	Ganesh	For good sleep & third eye/crown Chakra
Rock Salt	Remove black magic	Shiva	
Black Sesamine	Same as blue flowers	Same as blue flowers	Same as blue flowers
Red Chilies	Removes jealousy	Same as red flowers	
Lemons	Remove all problems	Kartike	All Chakras
Turmeric Powder	Same as yellow flowers	Same as yellow flowers	
Clear quartz crystal	Same as white flowers	Same as white flowers	
Amethyst	Same as blue flowers	Same as blue flowers	
Black tourmaline	Same as blue flowers	Same as blue flowers	
Rose quartz	For wealth and relationship	Any of the Laxmi Seed	For heart and solar Chakra
Coconut	For all problems	All Mantra	Necessary
Coconut lamp with bitter oil	For all problems	All Mantra	Crack coconut in ½ & make a lamp with oil
11 Lemon incenses stick	For all problems	Kartike	All Chakras
Camphor	For all problems	All Mantra	All Chakras
Peacock feather	For closing the Aura in the end.	Kartike	Use white flowers if feathers are banned

Process of Aura Cleansing:

✓ The first step in cleansing the Aura is to read the Aura carefully, study the blocks, dark patches, and if you see a major problem, ask the patient if he or she has any health problems of that particular area.

✓ Then study the size and activeness of all Chakras, speak to the patient about emotional blocks or problems which might have blocked the Chakra.

✓ Decide what material you will need for cleansing. Using extra material is advisable.

✓ Activate your hand and finger Chakra as per the process explained in 'Chakra'.

▶ Breathing Process:

✓ Ask the patient to concentrate on breathing throughout the process. When the patient breathes in, the stomach must come out and when he breathes out, the stomach goes in.

✓ The patient must take long and deep breaths, and leave the body loose.

✓ Your breathing pattern has to be the same.

▶ Releasing the blocks:

✓ Let the patient sit. Stand behind the patient and check for the swollen nerves in the head, especially behind the ears. It is not surprising find the blocks on the same spots behind right and left ear. Start massaging those blocks slowly in clock wise moments with your fingers chanting the Maha-Mirtunjay Mantra.

✓ Now place both your palms on the patient's shoulder joints. Ask the patient to keep his hands hanging down and chant the Maha-Mirtunjay Mantra eleven times. Ask him/her to concentrate on feeling the negativity flowing down from his or her fingers.

✓ If the patient is comfortable lying down, ask him or her to do so.

✓ Remind the patient to concentrate on the breathe and take deep breathes, and check whether he or she is taking proper breathes too.

✓ Keep the atmosphere light keep talking to the patient, crack a few jokes, let the Aura cleansing music play.

✓ Burn 'Hansa's Evils Eye Aura Oil'.

✓ Assure the patient that all will be fine.

✓ After every process, tell the patient you are already seeing the positive change in his or her Aura.

▶ The Method of Cleansing:

✓ Hold the material in your right hand. Keep the left hand open facing the sky. Check that you and your patient are breathing properly, place the right hand on the crown of the patient and start the cleansing process as shown under:

✓ In the first round: Start from the Crown Chakra chanting the corresponding Mantra, go down slowly to the left ear then go to the neck, move down to the left shoulder, go down to the left arm, follow this with the left thigh, down to the left knee to the left calf, moving to left foot then to right foot, from there go to right calf, up to right knee, right thigh, right palm, right hand, right shoulder, right neck, right ear, and back to the Crown Chakra.

✓ In the second round: Start from the Crown Chakra chanting the corresponding Mantra, go down slowly to the left cheek now move inwards, to left jaw, neck, left shoulder, left lung, left waist, left hip, left thigh, down to the left knee to left calf; then to the left foot followed by the right foot, from there go to the right calf, up to the right knee, right thigh, right hip, right waist, right lung, right shoulder, neck, right cheek and to the Crown.

✓ In the third round: Start from the Crown Chakra chanting the corresponding Mantra, go down from the right forehead, to the left eye, left lips, left chin, left throat, left chest, left nipple, left stomach left abdomen, left thigh, down to the left knee to the left calf, down to left foot then move to right foot, from there go to right calf, up to the right knee, right thigh, right abdomen, right stomach, right nipple, right chest, right shoulder, right chin, right lips, right eye, right forehead and up to the crown.

✓ In the fourth round: Start with the Crown Chakra chanting the corresponding Mantra, go down to the forehead, to the third eye, to the nose, the lips, the throat, the chest, the solar plexus, the navel, the genitals, inside both thighs, knee, calves, foot and come up through the same route to the crown.

✓ The fifth round will be similar to the third round.

✓ The sixth round will be same as the second round.

✓ The seventh round will follow the first round.

▶ **Channeling the Energy and Cleansing the Chakra:** After cleansing the body, move towards the Anus. Take the material five inches near the Chakra starting from the base Chakra moving towards the Crown from bottom to top. Make clockwise movements chanting the Mantra. Ask the patient to keep his or her attention on the base Chakra. During and after the cleansing, the patient will feel the Chakra rotating. If he or she feel no movements, then you must know that the Chakra is blocked and you will require to give more attention to that particular chakra.

✓ It is important to cleanse the solar plexus Chakra for women and emotional people.

▶ Cleansing the Aura:

✓ Start opening the Aura with flowers and corresponding Mantra by moving the flowers in clockwise direction. Keep your hands very close to the patient, at least within six inches of the patient's body as Aura is of the same length. Move downwards from the patient's left and upwards from the patient's right.

✓ Then cleanse the Chakra. After cleansing the Chakra, start the second round with some other material. Do not reuse any of the material.

✓ Use all material which need to be lit like burnt lamp made out of coconut shell, lemon flavor incense sticks, and camphor in the end, to burn out all negativities which may have arrived on the surface.

✓ Close and cleanse the Aura with peacock feather or any other feather. If use of feathers is banned in your country, then you may use any white coloured flowers.

✓ Do not use more chillies or more lit material for people who are short-tempered, as these items create more fire element in the Aura. Use one lit item instead.

✓ Use more chillies for people suffering due to jealousy; chillies are the best to remove jealousy.

✓ Cleanse the Mulaadhar (base) Chakra for those with suicidal tendencies. The best material to do so is fire substances like Ccamphor and lemon flavor incense sticks. The best Mantra for cleansing and activation of the base Chakra is 'Ganesh Mool Mantra'.

✓ Cleanse the Swadhisthan (sex) Chakra for those suffering from depression. The best material to do so are lemons. The best Mantra for cleansing and activation of the sex Chakra is 'Maha Mrityunjay Mantra'.

✓ Cleanse the Manipur (Navel) Chakra for those suffering from greed or jealous. The best material to do so is chillies. The best Mantra for cleansing and activation of the navel Chakra is 'Ganesh Mool Mantra'.

✓ Cleanse the Solar plexus Chakra is recommended for over emotional and sensitive people. The best material to do so is flowers. The best Mantra for cleansing and activation of the solar plexus Chakra is 'Laxmi or Vishnu Bij Mantra'.

✓ Cleanse the Anaahat (heart) Chakra of those suffering from fear or anger. The best material to do so is flowers. The best Mantra for cleansing and activation of the heart Chakra is 'Laxmi or Vishnu Bij Mantra'.

✓ Cleanse the Vishuddhi (throat) Chakra very well of the patient suffering from ill health and guilt. The best materials to do so are green leaves, lemon and blue flowers. The best Mantra for cleansing and activation of the throat Chakra are 'All Shiva Mantras'.

✓ Cleanse the Aangya (third eye) Chakra of people suffering from lack of attention and anger. The best materials to do so are salt, coconuts, incense sticks, camphor and white flowers. The best Mantra for cleansing and activation of the Third eye Chakra are 'All Shiva Mantras' and 'Kartike Mantra'.

✓ Cleanse the Sahastrar (crown) of the patient. All materials to do so are salt, coconuts, incense sticks, camphor and white flowers. The best Mantra for cleansing and activation of the crown are 'All Shiva Mantras'.

✓ Use all the materials starting from flowers and ending with fire rounds. Then close the Aura to make its protection outer layer stronger. This will end the Aura cleansing process.

2. Distance Aura Cleansing

Distance Aura cleansing is not 100% effective but can be done if there is no other alternative. Instead of the patient it can be performed on patient's:

✓ Used clothes.

✓ Photograph.

✓ Close family member, relative, or friend of the patient. This is only possible if the friend or family member thinks of the patient continuously during the process. Many Indian naturopathy doctors well-versed in the art of Nadi-Chikitsa can diagnose the illness of the patient by checking the pulse of his friend or family member, making them think about the patient.

✓ The Aura of the person can also be cleansed by sending him Aura protection material.

Many western psychics claim to clean the Aura on the phone, but I and my students after a deep research have come to a conclusion that Aura cleansing on phone is a fake claim and not possible.

Though talking to someone you love or respect can cleanse your Aura but professional cleansing is not possible on the phone.

3. Protection:

Giving protection to the patient is a better option than distance Aura cleansing. Different methods and materials can be used or worn by the patient or the person who is easily affected by negativity to protect him or her if Aura cleansing is not possible. This methods and materials can also be used by everyone wanting clean Aura and a clean mind.Here's how to ensure that your 'protection' is effective:

✓ Wearing different stones like amethyst, clear quartz, black tourmaline and evils-eye stone can protect the Aura but is not useful in cleansing the Aura. These stones need to be cleansed with salt water every week or else they will crack when they try to hold negativity more than their capacity. If these stones crack you must not use them, as after that they are of no use. The evil's eye stone is the most powerful amongst all stones to stop negativity. Black quartz helps in removing hurdles and negative effects of Saturn. Clear Crystal is good for people in artistic field, to calm down a person. But those suffering from cough or cold must should avoid wearing clear quartz. Amethyst is also very good for people having sleep problems, but lazy people should avoid wearing it.

✓ Wearing spiritual items like Panch Mukhi Hanuman Kawach, Durga Kawach, Taabiz, Bharav Raksha helps, but only after getting it energized.

✓ Chanting any of the Mantra Chapter for 108 times everyday also helps.

✓ Read books like Hanuman or Bharav Chalisaa and Rakshaa Stotra.

✓ Using Aura cleansing salts are also effective in Aura cleansing. There are different aromatic sea salts that are energized by different Mantras and rituals > Likewise, there are different flavors for different days of the week.

✓ Using Aura cleansing face packs are the best product to cleanse your Aura. It is prepared with herbs, and cleanses your Aura and makes you look younger.

✓ Take shower with more than three hundred energized and sanctified Rudraksh. This will also help in keeping your blood pressure in control. Hansaa mystic shop sells energized and sanctified original Rudraksh beads rosary for the above purpose.

✓ Meditating regularly listening to Aura cleansing meditation CD is also a very powerful method of cleansing as well as protecting your Aura from negativity.

✓   Taking a sunbath will also cleanse your Aura.

✓   Swimming or bathing in a sea or flowing water will help in cleansing Aura. Any flowing water like a river or sea is considered great cleanser of negativity from body and Aura, Sea water or bathing with sea salt is considered more powerful because as per our modern science, our body and our planet consist of 80% sea water. All the water running out of our system like sweat, urine or tears is salty. Every living being has breathed and lived very safely with a clean Aura in this salt water.

✓   Sea breeze is equally effective. Taking a walk by the sea also helps in cleansing the Aura.

✓   Being with nature, walking barefoot on grass, gardening are all good ways of keeping your Aura healthy.

✓   Creativity also keeps the Aura healthy

✓   Being with the kids also keeps the Aura healthy and fresh.

SECTION
6

1. Mantra

It is said in the scriptures that 'Manan Trayati iti Mantra'. That means the mind is Mantra.

There are many Mantras from various religions having various presiding deities and various meanings.

I have chosen, from experience, the best Mantra for Aura cleansing. The method on how to use them is given in the previous section of 'Aura cleansing'.

These Mantras can also be used for chanting at home for peace and prosperity.

▶ **Ganesh Mantra:**

✓ Ganesh Mool Mantra:

"Aum Gang Ganpateye Namah"

Meaning:

Aum Gang (the seed syllables of Ganesh) I bow down to Ganesh.

▶ **Shiva Mantra:**

✓ Shiva Panchakshar Mantra:

"Aum Namah Shivay"

Meaning:

Aum I bow down to Shiva who is all pervading the consciousness of everything.

This is the oldest and most powerful Mantra. It can be used for all types of Aura cleansing. People from different religions can do alternate Mantra, which have the same effect. A few Mantras are :

✓ Muslims can chant their Tasbi "**Allah Hoo Akbar**"

✓ Christians and Jews can chant "**Alleluia**" or "**Hallelujah**"

Meaning:

Let us Pray or Praise or if we take it literally boast the lord.

✓ Shiva Panchakshar with seed syllables (Saha Bij) Mantra:

"Aum Hrim Namah Shivay"

Meaning:

Aum Hrim (the seed syllables for Shakti and Laxmi) I bow down to Shiva.

✓ Shiva Maha-Mirtunjay Mantra:

"Aum Triambakam YajaMahe Sughandhim Pushti Vardhanam Urva Rukmiva Bandhanat Mirtyor Mukshi Ma-amritat Aum"

Meaning:

Aum O one with three eyes (one who can see all three tenses Past, present and future) I pray to thee, Make me smell good and holistically healthy, like a bird or cucumber (immediately and effortlessly) free me from the bondages of death but not from the nectar of immortality Aum.

✓ Maha-Mrityunjay seed syllables (Bij Mantra):

"Aum Houm Jhoum Saha Aum"

Chant the Maha-Mirtunjay Bij Mantra instead of Maha-Mrityunjay Mantra only if there is a difficulty in chanting Maha-Mrityunjay Mantra.

► Shakti Mantra:

✓ Siddha Kunjika Mantra:

"Aum Aim Hrim Klim Chamundaye Viche Aum"

✓ Baglamukhi seed syllables (Bij Mantra):

"Hilrim"

▶ **Laxmi & Vishnu Mantra:**

There are two Laxmi seed syllables (Bij Mantra)

✓ Laxmi seed syllables (Bij Mantra): *"Shrim"*

✓ Laxmi seed syllables (Bij Mantra): *"Hrim"*

✓ Vishnu seed syllables (Bij Mantra): *"Vim"*

▶ **Kartikeya**

✓ Kartikeya Mool Mantra:

> *"Aum Saravana Bhava"*

▶ **Shani:**

✓ Shani Mool Mantra:

> *"Aum Sham Shane Namah"*

✓ Shani Vedic Mantra:

> *"Aum Pram Prim Prom Saha Shane Namah"*

2. Guidelines of Aura Cleansing and Meditation Techniques:

1.Nadi Shodhan Pranayam:

~ Keep your back straight, head straight, eyes closed and shoulders relaxed; keep a smile on your face and drop your body weight on the ground that you are sitting on. Be sure that you are not crossing your hands or legs unless you are sitting cross leged in Sukh-Asana (crossed legs posture), or Padma-Asana (lotus posture).

~ Keep your right hand thumb on the right nostril, your index and middle finger in between the eyebrows where your third eye is placed and your right hand ring and little finger on your left nostril.

~ Your left hand must be on your left lap facing the ceiling open or in Chin Mudra i.e. the index finger lightly touching the thumb.

~ Remember that whenever you will breathe in, your stomach should come out and whenever you breathe out, your stomach goes in. This is a thumb rule.

~ Now we will start the first round. Block your right nostril by pressing it with your right hand thumb and very slowly breathe in through your left nostril.

~ Then block your left nostril by pressing it with your right hand ring and little finger and very slowly breathe out through your right nostril releasing it by loosening your right hand thumb.

~ After breathing out completely keep your left nostril blocked and very slowly breathe in through your right nostril.

~ Then block your right nostril by pressing it with your right hand thumb and very slowly breathe out through your left nostril by loosening your ring and little finger. This ends one round.

~ Second round block your right nostril and very slowly, breathe in through your left nostril.

~ Block your left nostril and very slowly breathe out through your right nostril.

~ After breathing out completely, keeping your left nostril blocked and very slowly breathe in through your right nostril.

~ Then block your right nostril and very slowly breathe out through your left nostril. This ends the second round.

~ Third round block your right nostril and very slowly breathe in through your left nostril.

~ Block your left nostril and very slowly breathe out through your right nostril.

~ After breathing out completely, keep your left nostril blocked and very slowly breathe in through your right nostril.

~ Then block your right nostril and very slowly breathe out through your left nostril. This ends the third round.

~ For the fourth round, block your right nostril and very slowly breathe in through your left nostril.

~ Block your left nostril and very slowly breathe out through your right nostril.

~ After breathing out completely, keep your left nostril blocked and very slowly breathe in through your right nostril.

~ Then block your right nostril and very slowly breathe out through your left nostril. This ends the fourth round.

~ For the fifth round, block your right nostril and very slowly breathe in through your left nostril.

~ Block your left nostril and very slowly breathe out through your right nostril.

~ After breathing out completely, keep your left nostril blocked and very slowly breathe in through your right nostril.

~ Then block your right nostril and very slowly breathe out through your left nostril. This ends the fifth round.

~ For the sixth round, block your right nostril and very slowly breathe in through your left nostril.

~ Block your left nostril and very slowly breathe out through your right nostril.

~ After breathing out completely, keep your left nostril blocked and very slowly breathe in through your right nostril.

~ Then block your right nostril and very slowly breathe out through your left nostril. This ends the sixth round.

~ To start the seventh round, block your right nostril and very slowly breathe in through your left nostril.

~ Block your left nostril and very slowly breathe out through your right nostril.

~ After breathing out completely keep your left nostril blocked and very slowly breathe in through your right nostril.

~ Then block your right nostril and very slowly breathe out through your left nostril. This ends the seventh round.

~ For the eight round , block your right nostril and very slowly breathe in through your left nostril.

~ Block your left nostril and very slowly breathe out through your right nostril.

~ After breathing out completely keep your left nostril blocked and very slowly breathe in through your right nostril.

~ Then block your right nostril and very slowly breathe out through your left nostril. This ends the eight round.

~ To start the ninth round, block your right nostril and very slowly breathe in through your left nostril.

~ Block your left nostril and very slowly breathe out through your right nostril.

~ After breathing out completely keep your left nostril blocked and very slowly breathe in through your right nostril.

~ Then block your right nostril and very slowly breathe out through your left nostril. This ends the Nadi Shodhan Pranayam.

~ Keeping your eyes closed, bring your right hand down, and relax, and see the flow of energy in your body. Get ready to chant 'AUM'.

2. AUM

~ The method of chanting Aum is that, we breathe in and breathe out as we chant a long 'Aum'. AUM is a combination of three sounds A U and M, the sound A and U will vibrate our torso and the humming sound of M will vibrate our head.

~ The proportion of chanting A and U will be 2/3 and the humming of M will be for 1/3 proportion.

~ Keep your back straight, head straight, eyes closed and shoulders relaxed; keep a smile on your face and drop your body weight on the ground that you are sitting on.

~ Your hands must be on your lap facing the ceiling open or in Chin Mudra i.e. the index finger lightly touching the thumb.

~ Ensure your hands or legs are not crossed unless you are sitting cross legged in Sukh-Asana (cross legged posture), or Padma-Asana (lotus posture).

~ Remember, when ever you breathe in, your stomach should come out and whenever you breath out your stomach should go in, as this is a thumb rule. Take a deep breathe in and with a big smile on your face, breathe it out.

~ Take a deep breath and relax your shoulders. Breathe out.

~ Take one more deep breathe in and keeping your body still and straight, breathe it out.

~ Take a deep breath in to chant 'AUM'.

~ Breathe in again 'AUM'.

~ One more time 'AUM'

~ Relax, keep your eyes closed and be ready for Aura Cleansing Meditation.

3. Aura Cleansing Meditation

This meditation is to cleanse and expand your Aura and Chakra at Alfa, Beta and Theta level. In this meditation we will play with sound.

The king of all Bij Mantra is 'RAM' in the Vedas. It is said that 'RAMETI ITI RAM' that which shines in me, my Aura is 'Ram'.

The English word Radiance or the Russian 'RA' that means "to shine" comes from the Sanskrit word 'RA'; and 'M' means in me.

The method of chanting "RAM" is we have to breathe in and breathing out we chant "R A M"

We have to press on the word 'RA' and 'M' must be pronounced silently and naturally, when we close your mouth.

When 'RAM' is chanted the whole body vibrates and the Aura expands and gets cured; all aliments of the body will also be cured.

If this meditation is practiced regularly for a period of 45 days with total faith then it can cure many small illnesses and phobias, for bigger problems, practice it for a period of six months regularly.

Be sure that we have no leather or black clothes on our body while we are meditating.

Best is to do wearing white light cotton clothes.

We will be still like a white marble statue throughout this Aura meditation session.

Let us sit or lie down comfortably, it is better that we sit with our back straight.

Take a deep breathe in and breathe out.

Relax your shoulders, close your eyes and keep a big smile on your face.

Take a deep breathe in and breathe it out.

Remember the rule: when you breathe in your stomach comes out and when you breathe out your stomach goes in.

Become aware of all the sounds in the surroundings.

Accept the sounds with total love.

Take a deep breathe in, and chant Ram breathing out. 'R A M'

You are in harmony with your surroundings.

Breathing in you will become aware of the weight of your body, and while breathing out you will feel the the total weight drop on the floor or the chair you are on.

Take a deep breathe and chant Ram breathing out. 'R A M'

Once again, when breathing in, you will become aware of the weight of your body, and breathing out a drop in the total weight on the floor or the chair you are on.

Take a deep breathe in, and chant Ram breathing out. 'R A M'

Relax more and more.

Let us become aware of our body. Bring your attention to your right foot, right calf, knee, thigh and hip. Then shift your attention to the whole right leg.

Take a deep breathe in and chant Ram breathing out. 'R A M'

Bring your attention to your left foot, left calf, knee, thigh and hip; shift your attention to the whole left leg.

Take a deep breathe in, and breathing out chant 'R A M'

Bring your attention to your genitals.

Take a deep breathe in, and breathing out chant 'R A M'

Bring your attention to your abdomen, stomach and lower back.

Take a deep breathe in, and breathing out chant 'R A M'

Bring your attention to your chest, lungs, heart and upper back.

Take a deep breathe in, and breathing out chant 'R A M'

Bring your attention to your shoulders.

Take a deep breathe in, and breathing out chant 'R A M'

Bring your attention to your right arm.

Take a deep breathe in, and breathing out chant 'R A M'

Bring your attention to your left arm.

Take a deep breathe in, and breathing out chant 'R A M'

Bring your attention to your throat.

Take a deep breathe in, and breathing out chant 'R A M'

Bring your attention to your chin, lips, jaws, teeth, tongue, cheek, nose, eyes, ears forehead and brain.

Take a deep breathe in and breathing out chant 'R A M'

Bring your attention to your whole body, your total body.

Take a deep breathe in and breathing out chant 'R A M'

You are in harmony with your body.

Become aware of your thoughts.

Good thoughts or not so good thoughts-do not label them, accept all your thoughts.

Take a deep breathe in and breathing out chant 'R A M'

You in harmony with your thoughts.

Become aware of your feelings.

Good feelings or not so good feelings accept all your feelings.

Take a deep breathe in and breathing out chant 'R A M'

You are in harmony with your feelings.

Our body is like a tree and the Aura or mind is like a creeper rotating around it.

Start rotating mentally around your own body in clock-wise direction from bottom to top.

Let your attention rotate around your feet.

Rotate around your calf.

Let your attention rotate around your knee and your thigh.

Let your attention rotate around your hip and anus, at the Mulaadhar Chakra.

Rotate the base Chakra (Mulaadhar Chakra) clock-wise.

Keeping your attention at the Mulaadhar Chakra, take a deep breathes chanting 'R A M'

Keep rotating the base Chakra (Mulaadhar Chakra) clock-wise.

Breathing in bring your attention to the Swadhisthan Chakra which is based at the genitals.

Rotate the genital Chakra (Swadhisthan Chakra) clock-wise.

Take a deep breathe in, and breath out chant 'R A M'

Keep rotating the genital Chakra (Swadhisthan Chakra) clock wise.

Breathing in, bring your attention to the Manipur Chakra, which is based at the Navel.

Rotate the Navel Chakra (Manipur Chakra) clock-wise.

Take a deep breathe in and breath out chant 'R A M'

Keep rotating the Navel Chakra (Manipur Chakra) clock wise.

Breathing in, bring your attention to the Anaahat Chakra, which is based at the heart.

Rotate the Heart Chakra (Anaahat Chakra) clock-wise.

Take a deep breathe in and breath out chant 'R A M'

Keep rotating the Heart Chakra (Anaahat Chakra) clock-wise.

Breathing in, bring your attention to the Vishuddhi Chakra which is based at the neck.

Rotate the Throat Chakra (Vishuddhi Chakra) clock-wise.

Take a deep breathe in and breathing out chant 'R A M'

Keep rotating the Throat Chakra (Vishuddhi Chakra) clock-wise.

Breathing in bring your attention to the Aangya Chakra which is based in-between the eyebrows.

Rotate the Third-eye Chakra (Aangya Chakra) clock-wise.

Take a deep breathe in and breathing out chant 'R A M'

Keep rotating the Third-eye Chakra (Aangya Chakra) clock-wise.

Breathing in, bring your attention to the Sahastrar which is based on the Crown.

Rotate the Sahastrar (Crown) clock wise.

Take a deep breathe in and breath out chanting 'R A M'

Keep rotating the Sahastrar (Crown) clock-wise.

From the crown bring your attention to the whole body.

Bring your attention to the space, which is six inches around your body, feel the heat of your Aura which is six inches around you.

Take a deep breathe in and breath out chanting 'R A M'

Become aware of the space in-between the top of your head and the ceiling,

Become aware of the total room that you are in,

By expanding our awareness we can expand our Aura.

Being aware of the room in which you are, take a deep breathe in and breath out chanting 'R A M'

Become aware of the building that you are in, expand the awareness.

Being aware of the building in which you are, take a deep breathe in and breath out chanting 'R A M'

Become aware of the state or province that you are in, expand more and more.

Being aware of the state or province in which you are, take a deep breathe in and breath out chanting 'R A M'

Become aware of the country that you are in.

Being aware of the country in which you are, take a deep breathe in and breath out chanting 'R A M'

Become aware of a football.

Become aware of our planet earth, expand more and more.

Being aware of planet earth, take a deep breathe in and breath out chanting 'R A M'

Become aware of the entire Universe, expand more and more.

Become aware of all the stars and planets.

Being aware of the total universe, take a deep breathe in and breathe out chant 'R A M'

(Pause)

Become aware of a small grain of sand.

Aum from Untruth lead me to Truth. From Darkness lead me to light. From Death lead me to Immortality.

Aum let everyone everywhere be happy. Let everyone everywhere be happy. Let everyone everywhere be happy.

Aum Shanti Shanti Shantihi:

Take a deep breathe in, and breath out to become aware of your body. Take another breathe in and become aware of your surroundings. Slowly and gradually, when you feel complete, you may open your eyes.

For placing the order for Aura cleansing material, more Aura meditation CD's and Aura cleansing training sessions, please contact:

Hansaa Mystic Shop

Ph: +91 22 9867495496

+91 22 9323297398

Email: hittesh@rudrakshpuja.com

hitteshguruji@gmail.com

Website: http.//rudrakshpuja.com

http.//hansaamystic.com

<u>Thanks</u>

I would like to sincerely thank all my Gurus who have given me this vast knowledge so I could share it with the world.

I would like to thank my publishers.

I would like to thank Pakhiji, my teacher for having 100% faith in my knowledge and helping me publish the book. Her confidence gave me the strength.

I would like to thank Smitha Mukherji for editing my book and making the English readable for you.

Last but not the least I would like to thank my family, especially my wife Nita Morjaria and Krishaal H. Morjaria for supporting me when I was writing this book.

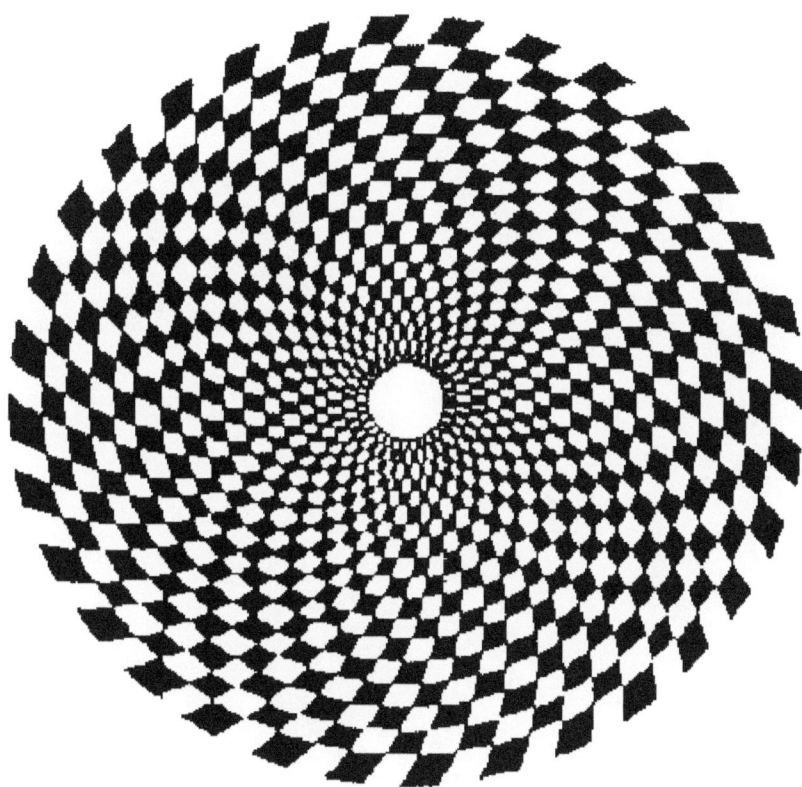

Pic. 8 of the Tratak wheel